No Place
Like Home

Operation Crufts

Sad Blue dog

ittle Helmand meeting
Lily his farm buddy

Char Badmashis

tch – if only he stayed this small!

No Place Like Home

A New Beginning with the Dogs of Afghanistan

Pen Farthing

EBURY
PRESS

3 5 7 9 10 8 6 4 2

First published in 2010 by Ebury Press,
an imprint of Ebury Publishing
A Random House Group company

The Random House Group Limited Reg. No. 954009

Addresses for companies within the Random House Group can be
found at www.randomhouse.co.uk

A CIP catalogue record for this book is available from
the British Library

The Random House Group Limited supports The Forest Stewardship
Council (FSC), the leading international forest certification organisation.
All our titles that are printed on Greenpeace approved FSC certified
paper carry the FSC logo. Our paper procurement policy
can be found at www.rbooks.co.uk/environment

Mixed Sources
Product group from well-managed
forests and other controlled sources
www.fsc.org Cert no. TT-COC-2139
© 1996 Forest Stewardship Council
FSC

Printed in the UK by CPI Mackays, Chatham, ME5 8TD

Printed and bound in Great Britain by Clays Ltd, St Ives PLC

ISBN 9780091928834

To buy books by your favourite authors and register for offers visit
www.rbooks.co.uk

Contents

Just Like Old Times

As the boom of the exploding rocket echoed round the eerily silent buildings, the brilliance of the ignited gunpowder lit up the night sky.

'Here we go again,' I said to myself, as I hurried across a short patch of grass towards a lone wooden building hidden in the shadows. I moved into a shallow crouch as I ducked my head in anticipation of the low opening I could see looming. Except I didn't crouch low enough.

'Ow!' My forehead had slammed into the top of the open doorway and I fell backwards on the wet grass in shock.

'That bloody hurt,' I said to nobody in particular, desperately rubbing what I knew would be a nice bruise in the morning.

For a moment I sat, semi-stunned, letting the pain slowly ebb away, but another loud, skyward explosion soon wrenched me back to the reality of why I was out here in the first place.

I rocked forwards on to all fours, trying to ignore the sensation of the wet grass soaking my trousers, and carefully stuck my head through the doorway. From this level it was blatantly obvious that I had not been crouching low enough.

'Idiot,' a small voice in the back of my head told me. 'Any dumb-ass would have realised this hadn't been built with a human in mind.'

I crawled into the poorly lit wooden room. 'Sorry, buddy, I should have got here sooner,' I said softly.

The wide, scared eyes of one of my dogs, Nowzad, were staring back at me in the gloom. He was curled into a tight ball with just his head pointing towards me; he looked like he was shaking. His short-docked tail was pulled in tight to his behind and what was left of his ears were pulled back against the sides of his head as another loud explosion rocked the small wooden shed. It sounded very close, even though I knew it was hundreds of feet above us.

'It's okay, mate: I'm here, buddy,' I reassured him again as I put one arm round his midriff, and using my free hand to turn up the volume of the radio hanging from a single nail above my head.

I figured the sound would drown out the noise of the now more frequent explosions, but as I heard the crackly, over-excited voice leading a countdown to what I knew would be even more loud bangs, I knew it was unlikely to do much good.

'*Ten, nine, eight, seven . . .*'

The annoying voice wasn't helping the throbbing pain in my head either. I closed my eyes and gently ruffled the outsides of Nowzad's roughly shorn-off ears – the most obvious sign of the life he had led until only a few months ago. I smiled as he pressed his ear back into my open palm. I rubbed it with even more enthusiasm.

'Just like old times, eh, Nowzad?' I chuckled, although really there was no funny side to that particular joke.

'. . . *three, two, one . . .*'

I thought the flashes outside were purely down to the barrage of explosions that was now going off somewhere above us, but as I shielded my eyes from the beam of light that was shining directly into my face, I realised that someone was pointing a torch inside the shed. Before I had a chance to respond, an arm reached in, extending a silver goblet of red wine into the gloom.

'Happy New Year, you two,' giggled my wife, Lisa.

'Happy New Year to you, too, honey,' I said, as I took a mouthful of wine and held the goblet that had been a wedding present, up in a mock salute.

Swallowing, I turned to Nowzad. 'And Happy New Year to you, Nowzie,' I said into his ear, as another year was ticked off and 2008 arrived. 'I know it doesn't feel like it at the moment, but you're safe. Nobody can hurt you now.'

It was the second year in a row that I had counted down to the changing of the year in the company of Nowzad rather than Lisa.

The setting couldn't have been more different, though.

This year we were in Nowzad's kennel in the garden of

Lisa's and my home in the Devon countryside. Twelve months earlier, Nowzad and I had been in a very different landscape: Afghanistan.

As a troop sergeant in the Royal Marines, I had been on a tour of duty with Kilo Company, 42 Commando. Along with the lads under my command, I had been posted to a so-called safe house in the desert town of Now Zad, deep in Helmand Province.

What had been safe about it had been a constant debate at the time. The mud-built compound (or 'forward operating base' to give it its proper title) crammed in amongst the narrow alleys and compounds of the closely built town had become our home over the freezing winter months of Christmas 2006. Our mission had been to provide security to the innocent Afghans who had wanted nothing more than to get on with their daily lives without the unwanted interference of the Taliban.

But that had meant we were often forced to spend hours manning our sentry positions in the freezing winter rain while the Taliban launched their mortars in our direction, which, inexplicably to most who had not served in the military I would imagine, provided some kind of distraction from the dull routine of life in the 'safe house'. In the run up to Christmas Day we were receiving incoming mortars on a daily basis although bizarrely the Taliban left us alone to enjoy the turkey and fresh potatoes that had been parachuted in by the RAF along with a much-needed ammo resupply.

It had proved to be an unreal experience in many ways: at no time had I ever thought I would be fighting in a country I had only ever seen portrayed in a Rambo film.

But we soon discovered that there was only so much 53 marines could do in holding the territory surrounding Now Zad from the Taliban, and that our lack of numbers meant we weren't really able to provide the security that the people so desperately craved.

I had found that incredibly frustrating.

But by a chance encounter in a dusty alley, I had ended up providing shelter and security for a select few of the town's stray dogs instead. Slowly, strangely and totally accidentally, I had become the Dog Warden of Now Zad.

A dog we had named Nowzad had been the first to be taken under my wing. I had encountered him during a routine clearance patrol in the alleyways outside the Marine compound, when I had come across a dogfight.

More than three years on from that fateful day, I can still vividly recall the sight and sound of the clash of snapping teeth and I still hear the ferociousness of Nowzad as he and another, larger dog did battle. Most of all, I can still hear the jeering Afghan Police egging the dogs on to attack each other.

I will never forget how angry I was, seeing two dogs attempting to rip each other to pieces in the name of entertainment, and I was determined to stop the people who had orchestrated it. It hadn't been the most sensible thing I had ever done, but I had barged into the centre of the action to break up the fight; besides we had the bigger guns.

The image of a scruffy, unwashed Afghan policeman tripping over his feet and landing squarely on his arse on the dusty ground as I pushed my way into the middle of the crowd still brings a smile to my face. And Nowzad had taken my intervention as his cue to make a run for it: as soon as a gap had appeared in the ring of frenzied spectators, both he and the other dog had charged away to the relative safety of the surrounding empty alleys and deserted, mud-walled buildings. The Afghan Police had been angry but there was little they could do seeing as they should never have left the security of our compound in the first place without permission. They had trudged off wearily while we watched over them, just in case the Taliban had decided to use that moment to attack, but thankfully it had never happened.

I had imagined that would be the last I would ever see of that Afghan fighting dog, but a few days later I had discovered Nowzad hiding in one of the empty buildings towards the western end of our compound. At first he hadn't been too receptive to me, to say the least. When I had approached him, he had let out a scary, nasty-sounding growl from a mouth of broken teeth; a sound that had sent me flinching backwards so fast it had been my turn to end up in a heap on the dust-covered ground.

Thankfully – for both of us – all it had taken to win him over were a few cardboard-flavoured military-issue biscuits.

One of my young marines came up with the idea of naming Nowzad after the battle-scarred town we were fighting over. It fitted perfectly. The deep scars down the right side of his face and under his chin were a continuous reminder of the harsh life he had already led.

In the days that had followed, I had put together a makeshift refuge for him, and in the space of a couple of months, it had somehow became a shelter-cum-sanctuary for five adult dogs and 14 puppies.

Nowzad had somehow spread the news of his good fortune, which included twice-daily meals of leftover military rations and a homemade shelter from the harsh Afghan winter nights, to some of his other four-legged friends.

There was RPG who was a scrawny youngster who tripped over his own legs as he madly challenged the grumpy Nowzad to play. Jena was an affectionate darkly tanned dog with piercing yellow eyes that we discovered tied with wire around her neck to a wooden stake by the local Afghan Police. The aim we assumed was that she would be mated by the hordes of stray dogs that roamed as a pack constantly around the outside of our compound scavenging for scraps or looking for a gap in the reinforced fence. The Afghan Police's plan was simple – the frightened dog tied to the post would produce more puppies and the stronger ones could be used for future dogfights.

We had not untied her soon enough and I had watched fascinated as Jena gave birth to eight pups on a freezing New Year's Eve several weeks later.

There was AK, who we had found lying injured near our makeshift dog pen, the telltale deep puncture wounds of a snake clearly visible on the back of her neck. Antibiotics and some TLC from the lads soon had her back on the road to recovery.

In complete amazement we had witnessed a scrawny unfed dog carry her pups in under the back gate, one pup at a time, to the safety of our compound. Without a second thought the white dirt-covered mum and her six pups had been added to our growing dog pound. It had been easy to come up with her name: Tali – short for Taliban, as who else but the Taliban would attempt to crawl in under our rear gate?

In many ways, Nowzad got me through my time in Afghanistan: he helped me every bit as much as I helped him. Being able to spend a few moments a day sitting and chilling with him in his homemade dog run had kept me sane through the rough times. He had been my five minutes of peace, the pilot of the magic carpet that had transported me to my life back home and a world where I could watch my dogs Fizz Dog and Beamer Boy running free on the beach, charging after each other into the surf as Lisa and I wandered along hand in hand. And I had made the cardinal sin. I had given Nowzad a trust in humans that we had no right to give. If I could not get him to safety when I left how could I just leave him to return to what I assumed would be a very short and harsh existence before he either died of starvation or from wounds suffered during a fight?

With the world seemingly falling to pieces around me, Nowzad had been the one constant I could count on. His stumpy tail would always wag like mad as I approached his DIY run at all hours of the day and night depending on my watch routine. He was always happy to see me – especially around feeding time when I would put a bowl of leftover military dumplings inside his run.

For a dog that had been beaten, bombed and starved, Nowzad could forgive very easily: he had never judged me if I was late or in a rush.

As he'd proven again, tonight.

The fireworks were gaining in intensity outside, but the loud pop music that was now blaring out of the radio was doing a grand job of drowning out the noise. There was something bizarre and slightly surreal about the frequent bursts of brilliant light from each explosion that danced through the open doorway. As Lisa and I sat in the dog run with Nowzad, we felt like we were sitting on the edge of the stage during a psychedelic illegal rave party.

'Even last year was quiet compared to this!' I yelled to Lisa above the loud bang of another firework, a shivering and still frightened Nowzad tucked firmly up against me.

'How many bloody fireworks are there?' I said.

'Some people have just got far too much money to burn,' Lisa replied, jokingly.

I had loved fireworks as a kid, even going as far as to make my own. I would carefully break down the ingredients from inside the rockets I bought from the local shop, separating them into the different piles of coloured gunpowder before redesigning my own, more powerful explosives. Probably not the most intelligent of ideas if I think about it, and there had been some close calls. Now, however, I really don't care for fireworks; I would much rather spend my money on a few beers or a decent meal out. And there is also the far from minor detail that they scare the living daylights out of my growing pack of dogs.

'How are the others coping?' I shouted to Lisa as the next round of sky rockets shattered into dazzling fragments above us.

'Fizz Dog and Beamer Boy don't mind them,' she yelled back.

That didn't surprise me. Fizz Dog, our own Rottweiler, and Beamer Boy, our UK-rescued Springer Spaniel, had been part of our lives for six years. Sudden loud noises had never really bothered them, which was helpful given that they had started their lives with us living near the end of the runway of the Royal Naval Air Station at Yeovilton. Without much fuss, both dogs had adapted easily to the noise of the Harrier Jump Jets as they screamed overhead, and the booming of the military firing range nearby. Together, we had all just grown used to it.

'And what about Tali?' I asked, guilty that for a moment I had forgotten all about the other dog, that I had met on the far side of the world in Helmand Province and now lived with us.

Half the size of Nowzad, Tali was a white, hairy ball of constant energy.

Tali was a survivor, of that I had no doubt. And on arrival in the UK, she had also proved better behaved in the house then her fellow refugee, Nowzad. So as the darkness had fallen this New Year's Eve, I had assumed that she would be happier indoors, and I had actually been more worried about Nowzad sitting in a dark kennel at the bottom of the garden while all hell broke loose around him. Now, however, I was having second thoughts.

'Where is she?' I asked Lisa, picking myself up from the cold floor.

'I left her under the coffee table with the TV turned up full blast on some quiz show,' Lisa replied as she reversed out of the kennel into the early-morning dampness. 'She was okay,' she added, but sounding now a little unsure.

Nowzad was, at that time, barred from entering the house in normal circumstances. But these weren't normal circumstances. As another rocket went off I looked at him shivering nervously. I couldn't watch him cower like this any more: I hadn't rescued him and brought him halfway across the world for this.

'Right, that's it,' I said, summoning all the authority I could muster: 'Lisa, Nowzad is scared stupid. I'm bringing him in to be with Tali. At least they can be scared together.'

'But he'll wee everywhere,' Lisa protested.

'Come on, honey,' I pleaded. 'We'll just watch him like a hawk.'

Lisa was stern-faced. 'It was you who thought it was a great idea to bring him all the way back from Afghanistan,' she said, before a giggly, wine-induced little smile broke out. '*You'll* have to watch him like a hawk.'

CHAPTER ONE

All Change

The New Year arrived eight days after we collected Nowzad and Tali from the quarantine centre where they'd spent the compulsory six months in isolation since arriving in England from Afghanistan.

To say it had been an eventful time was the understatement of the century. In the space of those eight days, it felt like our lives had been turned upside down.

We had slowly counted down the six months on our calendar, although we didn't need to pencil in any reminder as their release date was engraved on our minds. When the due date finally arrived there was no official letter, just a confirmation phone call to say that the vet had given the dogs the final all-clear and that was it: quarantine for our Afghan four-legged friends was over.

After months of making the long drive from the West Country up to the quarantine centre on the outskirts of London, it was great to have Nowzad and Tali released. The facilities inside the centre were basic, but the staff couldn't have done more to make both dogs feel at home. However, it had been frustrating not being able to take the pair of them out for a long, lung-busting walk or chuck a ball around in the park; not that Nowzad or Tali were the ball-fetching type.

Above all, I had wanted them living at home with Lisa, me and the other two dogs: I was looking forward to them becoming part of our pack. We had our favourite walks round our neighbourhood that we were planning on introducing the pair of them to, and the longer outings on Dartmoor when time allowed.

As we'd begun counting down the days to the end of the quarantine period, Lisa and I had both become quite nervous, as well as excited. Once the Afghan Two were out, that was it. Whatever happened we would have to make things work; I couldn't just take them back.

But then, as always, our employers put a spanner in the works. Lisa was, like me at that time, a member of the Forces: she was a WREN in the Royal Navy. As members of the Armed Services, both of us knew we were liable to be asked to move home at any time. Sure enough, with unbelievably bad timing, Sod's Law came into effect just as we were getting ready to collect the dogs.

I had been promoted: nearly a year after returning from Afghanistan my performance had finally been assessed and my commanding officers had, apparently, approved of the way I had led the lads through our time in Helmand Province. The report my old boss had given me had persuaded the powers-that-be that after seven long years as a sergeant it was time for a promotion. So I now held the rank of Colour Sergeant.

But it also meant I needed to be living closer to work, on the south coast near Exmouth. We'd be moving around 50 miles from our current quarters to a house on an estate linked to the base.

It was good news in the long term, but bad news in the very short term. Until then we'd been treating the dogs' release on December 24th as the perfect early Christmas present. But now our plans to accommodate them at our old home fell by the wayside in an instant.

Although nobody else had been counting I had, in nearly 20 years of serving as a marine, moved 14 times. Both Lisa and I longed to finally call somewhere home but it wasn't going to happen yet, that was for sure. We had to move to our new house in Devon on the day before, December 23rd, which gave us precisely 24 hours to not just move all our belongings, but also to prepare our new home for the arrival of two new dogs, as well as our existing pair. It had been a pretty hectic time, one way or another.

The quarters we'd been moved to were comfortable enough and, most importantly, had a fair-sized garden at the back. From the new house one could just about see the coast and on a good day, you could certainly smell the salty tang of the sea on the winds blowing in from the estuary.

Deciding where everything went in the new house was down to just one person. And, of course, that wasn't me. So while Lisa exercised her female prerogative and arranged the rooms as she wanted them, I stayed out of the way and devoted most of my time to building the two kennels that could accommodate our four dogs during the day – when we weren't around – and also house Nowzad at night, while he learnt to be house-trained. The decision had been made that he would sleep outside for the time being, while Tali would have a bed in the kitchen where we could at least limit her wandering into the rest of the house. Fizz Dog and Beamer Boy slept upstairs.

During their six months in quarantine, we had kept Tali and Nowzad in separate kennels. We'd done this for a couple of reasons. Firstly, we weren't sure whether Nowzad wanted a bunkmate and, secondly, we were also extremely mindful of the fact that neither dog had been neutered. We didn't want to be responsible for bringing even more unwanted puppies into the world, so had to do something about it. As with everything else, it hadn't been easy getting the job done and we only managed to get Nowzad and Tali neutered towards the end of their six-month quarantine, after acquiring a special DEFRA permit to allow a dog in quarantine to be operated on.

During their harsh former existence as strays of Helmand, Nowzad and Tali had obviously known each other as part of my Now Zad pack. The six months apart during their enforced quarantine didn't seem to bother them at all. They resumed their friendship as we left the quarantine facilities with a quick sniff of each other, and that was it.

Both Lisa and I let out sighs of relief; it was one less thing to worry about.

The kennels were fairly expensive models that we had ordered from a dog show the previous November. They resembled large garden sheds, and were insulated from the damp ground and fully waterproofed. A fenced dog run was attached to one side of each, enclosed by prison-style bars on two sides to allow the residents plenty of fresh air and the opportunity to watch the world go by. However, given that we lived in a pretty normal house on a pretty normal housing estate, the only bit of the world that was usually going by were the bin men who came once a week and the postman who came six days a week. Nothing very exciting.

The most interesting intermittent sight was, however, next door's cat, which had immediately discovered that he had the ability to drive Fizz Dog completely round the twist. I had noticed the cat on Day One. The playful cat had been perched delicately on the top of the dividing fence, sitting there with a 'you-can't-get-me' look written all over his face as Fizz Dog had barked and jumped up at him in vain.

The cat had also been there, watching me, as I put the finishing touches to the sheds on Christmas Eve. He, in turn, was being watched by most of our recently doubled-in-size canine contingent.

'I wouldn't think about falling in here, if I was you,' I said to him as I sat on the roof of one of the kennels, with a glance towards Nowzad who was propped up against the washing-line post surveying his new surroundings, and probably wondering what the hell was going on. 'He wouldn't even bother to chew.'

Lisa and I hadn't had time to worry about whether or not Nowzad was going to take to his new kennel. I had certainly worked on the assumption that whatever it was like, it would be positively palatial compared to the ruined Afghan outhouses that he had been living in for most of his life.

In fact, Nowzad had been completely laid-back about his surroundings when we'd let him out of the van after picking him and Tali up from the quarantine centre, and he went through the garden gate as if he'd done it a hundred times before.

His lack of concern was good news in more ways than one, as it meant he was feeling safe and happy. And, in particular, it also meant he wasn't bothered by the fact that I had cut a few corners in constructing his new home: dumped unceremoniously next to Nowzad while I had been finishing off the kennel was an overflowing bag of screws and nails that had arrived with the kit and should probably have been part of the finished structure.

'Don't tell Lisa, buddy,' I had said as I slid from the roof of the kennel and landed gently on the lawn. 'What she doesn't know won't hurt her,' I added, as I scooped up the bag of what I hoped were non-essential fixings and dropped them in the dustbin.

Nowzad had just followed me with his eyes. I knew I could rely on him not to give the game away.

*

As if bedding them into their new life hadn't been enough of a challenge, Nowzad and Tali also had to fit in with our other two dogs.

Lisa and I had got our first dog in 2001, just a month after we had been married. As a kid, I had had a dog called Shep, but being a youngster, I couldn't really remember too much about him. But dogs had always been part of Lisa's family, so it seemed natural to follow tradition.

Having a dog was something we'd talked about vaguely even before we'd got married. We had not really given choosing the right pet much thought and had bought our first dog from a breeder in Manchester. Looking back, we were naive in the extreme and didn't research it in the way we should have done. At the time, we knew nothing about puppy farming and some of the other sinister stuff that goes on in the canine world. But we were delighted by the dog we chose, a Rottweiler called Fizz, or 'Fizz Dog', as we liked to call her.

She'd been a challenge in many ways, but mainly because of her inherited obsession with chasing squirrels, or indeed any other animal. As a result, taking Fizz Dog for a walk was a perilous undertaking. She simply couldn't be let off the lead.

It had been when we'd collected Fizz Dog from her breeder that we'd been told about her heritage as a squirrel catcher: "Er mum's a right good 'un at catching them little tree rats,' the breeder had told us proudly as we collected our young pup. We had smiled nicely and ignored her.

'Like she would *want* to chase squirrels . . .' Lisa had cooed as she stared into the melting-chocolate eyes of the innocent-looking puppy.

Just how wrong could somebody be? Once she was old enough to go out for a decent walk, Fizz Dog had immediately proven that she was without question a chip off the old block. In fact, she only had to sniff a squirrel from 200 yards away and she would be off.

And, as she grew up, Fizz Dog had revealed that it wasn't just squirrels that she enjoyed chasing. Any animal would do, which was why if there was just the slightest possibility of livestock anywhere near us then Fizz Dog was grounded. In the early days, it was all we could do to hold on to her, while we scolded and attempted to drag her tensed body in the opposite direction as she howled in short, sharp screams of frustration at not being allowed to hunt her prey. Her high-pitched squeals would draw looks from passers-by, as it sounded as though we were secretly torturing her with electrodes as we dragged her away.

'It's okay, she's friendly really!' I would shout to people whilst smiling sincerely, my arms bulging as I used every ounce of power to keep her under control.

But otherwise Fizz Dog was a great companion, a dog that loved human company, children especially. Lisa used to take her into the gym in Yeovil with her when she was stationed there, and Fizz Dog loved nothing more than greeting the kids as they finished their swimming lessons and learned to sit to attention as they all came skipping out of the changing rooms, waiting for their hugs and cuddles. Lisa would watch over her but she had little to worry about as the kids pulled and prodded at Fizz Dog. She genuinely loved the attention.

Much as Fizz Dog enjoyed human company, however, we soon sensed she needed a dog pal.

Since getting her, Lisa and I had become supporters of an independent animal rescue centre in Somerset, Happy Landings, which was close to where we lived. Reading their monthly newsletter could put a smile on your face and reduce you to tears at the same time.

I hadn't really thought about it until then, but I was constantly struck by mankind's inhumanity towards the animal it likes to call its best friend. Some of the things I heard that the staff at Happy Landings had had to deal with made me angry and sick to the stomach.

So I had to agree without hesitation when Lisa said one night, as she put down a copy of the centre's latest newsletter: 'I think we should give a rescue dog a home.'

Lisa did all the ground work in finding a suitable companion for Fizz Dog. Sadly Happy Landings didn't have a dog that was compatible with our Rottie, but eventually we found a homeless Springer Spaniel that the rescue centre staff thought was called Beamer or Beamo or something like that but they were not quite sure. He had been taken in at an RSPCA shelter.

We knew how important it would be that our two dogs got on, so Lisa had taken Fizz Dog along to meet and socialise with Beamer Boy (as Lisa now called him) in one of the shelter's specially built enclosures. Luckily, they had got along brilliantly, chasing each other round and round in circles with no sign of aggression.

We had a few formalities to go through to convince the RSPCA that we were fit and proper owners. The rescue centre home checker wanted to know whether we would give Beamer Boy plenty of exercise, and had been fairly satisfied when Lisa informed him that as we were both physical-training instructors in the Armed Forces, Beamer Boy would not go short of a walk or two.

The story of how most stray and abandoned dogs end up in the care of rescue shelters is never normally made public and so while we had no clear guidance on Beamer Boy's past, one of the kennel girls did whisper to Lisa that it was something to do with him being left alone on a boat. I hadn't really understood why they could not tell us his past history; I assumed that it was to prevent us treating Beamer Boy too differently or maybe even seeking out the previous owner.

It had been Lisa's choice to get Beamer Boy. I was tied up with work at the time and hadn't been able to go and see him with her the first time. But she had taken lots of photographs that had made me smile as I had flicked through them on our computer screen.

Beamer Boy's playful, endearing face filled the screen.

His coat was straggly and unkempt; white with occasional jet black patches. His head was a mask of black except for a lone white stripe running from his forehead to the tip of his nose. His large, floppy ears were covered in black matted hair and desperately needed a trim.

But I agreed with Lisa that he was quality and we hadn't needed to discuss it any further. If Lisa was happy to give Beamer Boy a home, then I was too.

This time, it was Lisa who had been tied up with work on the day it had been agreed that we would collect him, so I had travelled to the re-homing centre in Weston-super-Mare. As I had stood in the waiting room waiting to be introduced to our new dog, I had felt overwhelmed by all the posters and information sheets on the walls:

'Is your dog micro chipped?'

'Have you neutered your dog?'

'Regular worming – what you should know.'

'Has your dog invited unwanted guests into your home – fleas?'

Owning a dog really was a big responsibility, so what about two of them? Little did I know that one day owning two dogs would be the least of my worries...

A young girl had appeared with a small, timid black-and-white Springer with a tennis ball lodged firmly in his teeth. His tail was wagging furiously as if he assumed he was going for a walk, which he was, of course, in a way: a long one.

'Here he is,' the young girl had said happily and, to my

surprise, the receptionist just handed me Beamer Boy's lead.

'There you go,' she said as I took hold of it. 'Your wife completed all the paperwork last time she was here.' I had imagined there was going to be more to it than that.

As I stepped out, Beamer Boy trotted alongside me as if he didn't have a care in the world. And I didn't know it at the time, but I reckon that was the moment my interest in dog rescue began.

Little could I have imagined where it would take me.

When I sat down and thought about it, I realised I had not really thought about the intricacies of owning four dogs. As Lisa reminded me with annoying regularity, I was probably taking on more than I could handle, especially when two of those dogs had never been house-trained or ever taken for a walk on a lead before. Something I had not really considered, I had to grudgingly admit.

We introduced the four of them for the first time at Lisa's father's farm in Wiltshire, where we'd left Fizz Dog and Beamer Boy while we'd headed up to the quarantine centre outside London to collect Nowzad and Tali. We had our concerns, of course, especially about Nowzad. But we'd been hopeful it would be fine, especially given the natures of our other two dogs.

Getting all four dogs together for the first time had been nerve-racking but, much to our relief, Fizz Dog's and Beamer Boy's meeting of Nowzad and Tali had been a bit of a non-event, as they'd welcomed the new arrivals with barely a second glance.

Ever since we have had them, Fizz Dog and Beamer Boy have been amazing in their ability to welcome all and sundry into their lives. I had really hoped they wouldn't be fazed by the two new weary arrivals and, sure enough, they weren't. Just to be on the safe side, we'd kept them all on a lead, but our fears of all-out dog war had not materialised; instead, they'd just greeted each other in typically canine fashion, by sniffing each other's bums.

As I watched them, I couldn't help thinking how glad I was that as humans we used the good old-fashioned hand-shake as a way of introduction.

'See, instant dog karma,' I had said to Lisa as she stood nervously by, holding on to Nowzad's lead with an iron grip.

'Early days, know-it-all,' she'd replied, obviously not too convinced.

Lisa's scepticism was fair enough, especially where Nowzad was concerned. She hadn't spent the time I had with him and when she'd first met him at the quarantine, he'd actually tried to bite her. Not that it had fazed Lisa, but the jury was still very much out as far as she was concerned.

The four dogs sat quietly through the car journey back from the in-laws' farm to our new house, and I think the way the dogs behaved on the journey home temporarily lulled us into a false sense of security. We both forgot that two of our pack were products of a society and a way of life that was completely at odds with our own, but we soon snapped out of our complacency when Nowzad wasted no time in making his mark on our new home. Literally.

I had been outside sorting the dogs out when I had heard the ominous shout coming from inside the house: 'Nowzad, NO!'

Three seconds later and a fleeing Nowzad had shot out of the back door, closely followed by a not-too-impressed Lisa as she directed him on to the grass.

'What are you gawping at?' Lisa yelled at me as I stood there smirking, watching the scene unfold. 'Get in there and clean it up!'

I stepped into the kitchen to see what Nowzad had left behind after merrily cocking his leg on the corner of a kitchen unit: a large, yellowish puddle.

Even though I had gone to a lot of trouble to erect the kennels, deep down I had been hoping to bring both the Afghan dogs into the house to live within a short time of their arrival. Nowzad had immediately scuppered that plan. He seemed happy marking everything as his. He had weed on everything in Afghanistan and he had been quite happy to wee on everything in quarantine. So we were under no illusions that anything would change when he was introduced to our house, which was why Lisa had been adamant from the beginning.

Whenever I even suggested that, long term, he might one day live full-time in the house, I had been greeted by the same steely gaze.

'He is not living in the house,' Lisa would say.

'Yes, dear,' I would reply.

There was no way Lisa was going to have him living indoors if that was the way he was going to carry on. Sadly, he had ensured that the newly installed kennels would have at least one permanent resident, to begin with anyway.

But after seeing how scared Nowzad was as the fireworks continued to sound in the New Year, it was decided there and then that Nowzad would sleep indoors in the kitchen, and spend his daytime hours outside in the painstakingly erected kennel until we could trust him full-time in the house.

On current form, I didn't think that would be for a while yet.

CHAPTER TWO

One Step at a Time

The image on the television screen was simply too good to be true. The American dog trainer and renowned 'dog whisperer', Cesar Millan, was walking his large and beautifully groomed pack of dogs without a single lead in sight and, it seemed, not a care in the world. In his laid-back Spanish-Californian drawl, he was explaining how any dog owner could enjoy this kind of relationship with their best friends; that anyone could enjoy a relaxing country walk like this.

I laughed at the screen. 'I wish.' I didn't even want to imagine the carnage that would ensue if we ever went out on a walk with our pack running free like that.

We had begun taking Nowzad and Tali for a walk almost immediately they had arrived with us at Christmas. Our first walk had been on a nearby beach, where, despite being kept on leads, the pair of them had enjoyed their freedom, even though they had been more interested in the hordes of other dogs being taken for a walk by their owners.

Walking the estate and the nearby footpaths and parks was no different. Still, we had to deal with other people and, in particular, other dogs. I began by simply walking up and down the roads on the estate on which we lived. It wasn't the busiest of places, but that didn't matter. Nowzad would snarl and lunge at whomever and whatever caught his eye: any dog that appeared within 100 yards of him was the enemy and, if one appeared, it was a hell of a job restraining him. Distracting Nowzad with treats was a non-starter, too, as he simply was not interested. He had better things to occupy his attention.

Each time I took him out, I had visions of what would happen if he ever did break free. With the approach of a loose dog, I would see the hackles on Nowzad's spine rise in anticipation. He would then thrash and jerk on his lead, and pulling and dragging him in the opposite direction was a mission in itself. Thankfully, he would eventually succumb to my exertions and be reluctantly pulled away, his head still bent round in the opposite direction from his body as he continued to try and eyeball the unwitting dog that had strayed into his personal space. It wasn't pleasant, for me or the other passers-by.

Tali, however, was constantly on the lookout for anything that moved. The moment she registered something, she would want to chase and catch it, and then definitely eat it if we gave her the chance; something we were not going to do. She really would chase anything: leaves blowing in the wind, rubbish bags and, particularly, other animals.

She really, *really* wanted to chase other animals. And she was well equipped to do so. Even with her short legs she had the speed of a gazelle and she had a good chance of catching anything.

I had already learned that it was a tough job keeping up with her. I had always prided myself on my ability to keep pace with Fizz Dog when she wanted to sprint on the lead, both of us tearing hell-for-leather across Dartmoor with a happily free-running Beamer Boy keeping pace.

'I wouldn't have a chance of keeping up with you, though, would I, Tali?' I would say to her as she strained to chase a bird she had spotted over half a mile away. So we had taken the precaution of buying both dogs full body harnesses as well as good, strong collars and leads. Not that they were foolproof methods of keeping them under control.

Tali had already proved that slipping her collar was a simple Paul Daniels magic trick for her; she had it down to two seconds and no struggling. She hadn't escaped out of her full body harness yet, but I didn't doubt her Houdini-like abilities and was sure she'd come up with a way of wriggling out of that eventually.

Nowzad was another matter, however. If he ever escaped it could have dire consequences not just for any person or other dog that he took a dislike to, but for him – and for me. It would only take a moment for him to undo all that I had spent trying to achieve.

As a result of both dogs' inclinations, we'd taken two practical decisions early on.

First, walking Nowzad and Tali on the pavements and footpaths round our house couldn't be our main form of exercise for the dogs so, for now at least, the beach had to become our dog-walking venue of choice.

A problem with using the beach was that the local council only allowed dog walkers on it during the winter. Come the summer, the sand-castle-building brigade took over the golden sands once more. We'd cross that bridge when we came to it.

The beach wasn't the most convenient place to get to as it involved a short drive to get there. It also was a real hassle loading all the dogs in the van just so we could go for a semi-mellow walk at the other end. But it was worth it – usually.

The beach walks worked for our old dogs as well as our new ones. Fizz Dog loved it for one simple reason. As there were no squirrels or sheep for her to eat, she was allowed to run leadless. Once released she would tear up and down the beach, her sleek body working effortlessly as she chased Beamer Boy in the soft sand – until distracted by a passing dog.

'It's okay, she just wants to say hello,' I would have to yell, as yet again a worried dog owner would scoop up their inevitability smaller dog from what they assumed was an angry, uncontrolled Rottie intent on devouring their precious pooch. But all Fizz Dog wanted to do was sniff them, dance around a bit and then charge off again, normally followed by her new four-legged friend.

Having Fizz Dog off the lead was a real benefit now that our pack had grown to four dogs, as it meant I could hand over Tali's reins to Lisa. As both of us walked through the sand with our two refugees, occasionally calling Fizz Dog or Beamer Boy back to run circles round us, we could attempt to work the two Afghans on the lead and do some kind of training. We always made sure we had bulging, treat-filled pockets we could dip into to reward both dogs on the rare occasions they actually listened to what we were saying.

'Are you sure they understand English?' Lisa asked one day, as Tali failed yet again to sit, after the tenth time of us telling her to.

'Let's hope they do,' I replied. 'We don't speak any Pashto.'

Of course, we couldn't get to the beach every day. So our second practical decision was that if there was only one of us around to take the dogs for a walk, then Lisa or I had to take them in two shifts.

We'd come to this conclusion one evening after a particularly exhausting workout in which all four dogs had pushed us to the limits of our tolerance.

'Sod this for a game of soldiers,' I had said as I slumped, exhausted, on the sofa. 'One of us can't take all four dogs out on our own,' I continued, as if Lisa hadn't already worked that out herself.

'No shit, smart arse,' she had replied. 'And just remember it was your idea to get four dogs.'

'It'll be all right,' I had replied in my most confident

voice. 'We'll get them trained in the end. We just need a bit more time.'

Lisa had simply raised her eyebrows in reply.

I recognised Nowzad's body language immediately.

What was left of his cropped ears was pressed tightly against the side of his head and his stumpy tail was firmly clamped to his backside. He was afraid of something. But what?

'What's the problem, Nowzie?' I said, kneeling down and ruffling the hair on his back.

Lisa and I had decided to take the dogs along one of our favourite walks that would eventually involve cutting back down a narrow country lane, a few hundred yards from home. There were several of these lanes nearby and they all made what we thought were ideal dog-walking locations. They were more secluded than most of the other pathways and during the spring and summer, in particular, the trees lining the paths would sway gently in the wind as their long droopy branches hung over our heads like a canopy, keeping the hot sun off us all.

We had come to a stop at the entrance to a narrow foot-path that threaded itself through the woods, the overhanging branches still stripped bare as spring was still another two months away. The tall, bare trees that lined both sides of the track created a kind of wall. Nowzad had halted and was pulling away heavily on the lead. It was clear he didn't want to go down the path.

At first it made little sense. For Beamer Boy, the entrance to the footpath meant he was already straining against his lead as he knew he would be allowed to run free down its entire length. For Fizz Dog, she knew it meant she got the chance to sniff under every bush and shrub as we walked along the lane in the hope that a squirrel might be sitting there unawares.

But Nowzad was having none of it – he really wasn't happy at all as we started off down the path. As we walked, Nowzad would slow and then suddenly dig in and root himself to the spot, almost ripping my arm from its socket as I unwittingly carried on walking forward.

'Come on, Nowzad,' I said once more, trying to coax him into the narrow alley. But again he was having none of it. I stopped and looked ahead and then back at Nowzad.

'What is it, mate? What do you see?' I said softly, crouching down by his side.

Tali just stood motionless to one side of us. She, too, looked a little apprehensive, although not as much as Nowzad. It was then that the penny dropped.

I suddenly thought of the network of narrow, mud-walled alleyways that criss-crossed their home town of Now Zad. I remembered picking my way along them as the lads of K Company and I carried out our regular patrols. I recalled how hemmed in you could feel in them, how you never knew who or what lay round every corner.

As the images flooded back to me, I realised Nowzad, too, was on the other side of the world again: 'You see Afghanistan, don't you, buddy?'

As I crouched down alongside him, speaking softly to him to reassure him, I realised something that hadn't struck me before. I had visited a few towns and villages in Helmand, and there had been stray dogs in most of them. Yet those strays had always congregated in open spaces and on street corners: I had never really seen any of them in the mud-walled alleyways. It was as if they sensed they were no place for dogs, especially when the Taliban and us were likely to start shooting at each other down them at a moment's notice.

I had no way of knowing it for sure, but I wondered now if Nowzad had been in one of those alleyways once when all hell had broken loose, and he didn't want to risk going down this pathway in case there was more of the same waiting for him. He clearly wanted to find a way off the path as he was looking from side to side as if trying to suss out an escape route. There wasn't one. We would have to backtrack and re-walk the roads we had just come down.

'It's okay, buddy, we need the exercise anyway,' I reassured him as we promptly about-turned to start the long route home.

'Nothing's easy with these two, is it?' I remarked to Lisa as she caught up with us around the corner from the alley.

This wasn't the only example of behaviour where the Afghan dogs differed from our English ones. We had also noticed that whilst Fizz Dog and Beamer Boy bounced round the garden in anticipation of an up-coming walk, our two resident Afghans would stand motionless by the gate as we fitted their Halti harness. They wouldn't move until the gate was opened and we were away on our walk. Currently they didn't get excited about the prospect of a good walk – to them I guessed it was another part of their current daily routine which they were adjusting to.

Life for an Afghan stray was a constant hunt for food and a fight against the elements – there wasn't much else to get excited about and I had rarely seen an Afghan dog just playing. We really hoped that these dogs would soon learn how to enjoy themselves and just chill. That was the cunning idea, anyway.

Taking the dogs for a walk together had become the closest thing me and Lisa had to a date these days. Now that we had moved, her day involved a 90-minute drive and, bizarrely, a ferry crossing just to get to work. She then had to do the same thing again at the end of the day. It meant that she was leaving home in the small hours of the morning, and she would often tell me that the ferryman had to tap on the window of the car to wake her up during the unloading phase of the crossing.

When she got home each night, I would be waiting for her with the dogs. She'd come in, drop her small day sack and hold out her hand to receive the two leads I had ready so that we could all go out together for a walk, before the frenzy of feeding time loomed as we arrived back home, 40 minutes later.

Normally, I would take Nowzad's lead in my right hand

and Tali's in my left and Lisa would walk Fizz and Beamer. One of the best bits of advice we'd received had been about the benefits of walking Nowzad with a Halti lead, which secures round the dog's muzzle. It made it easier to steer him and also prevented him from hurting himself when he pulled on the lead sharply, as he did often. And it now, thankfully, made the plastic muzzle that we'd made him wear early on for walks redundant.

The Halti didn't cure all his problems, of course. He still wanted to fight every dog he didn't know on the planet; although why he had not attempted to fight Fizz Dog and Beamer Boy during their first meeting I could only guess at. Maybe it was they smelt of me or me of them and Nowzad had already gotten used to that during my quarantine visits; maybe this pack idea really did work and Nowzad was happy to follow my lead. I didn't know for sure but I was just grateful that their first meeting had passed by without incident. And it was easier to get him away from the inevitable confrontations now. It was a small mercy, but I was thankful for it.

CHAPTER THREE

Fish Out of Water

The house was still in semi-darkness as I walked, bleary-eyed and bare-footed, out of the bedroom and padded my way down the stairs.

I had hardly set foot in the hallway when I felt a large, lukewarm and slightly squishy lump under my foot. I knew immediately what it was.

'LISAAA!' I yelled up the stairs.

She appeared almost immediately, flying down to see me as if I had just stabbed myself.

'What the hell's wrong?' she demanded.

The instant she saw me standing on one foot, my other foot gingerly held up as if I was performing some weird sort of Morris dance, the look of concern on her face gave way to a big grin.

'I have dog crap between my toes,' I said. 'And it is not bloody funny.'

Tali had adjusted well to life indoors, and had demonstrated some kind of awareness of what she should and shouldn't do. She was a dainty little madam, really, and quite house-proud with it, even though – as I had just discovered – she was prone to leaving the odd surprise in the mornings.

After I had cleaned myself and the mess up, I found her lying on the sofa in the living room, curled up as if she didn't have a care in the world. Which she probably hadn't.

Lisa was not amused by *this*, however. She had berated Fizz Dog and Beamer Boy many times over the years, telling them that our lovely dark green sofa was *our* domain and not theirs. During the early days of living with Fizz Dog, forgetting to shut the living-room door when we went out would always mean we came back to find a curled-up, sleeping Rottweiler, her solid head resting on the arm of the sofa as if about to watch a Sunday afternoon movie, dog drool staining the soft material covering the arm where she had dribbled in her sleep.

'Oops, you caught me,' would be written all over her black-and-tan sleepy face, her stumpy bob tail wagging like mad as Lisa would stoop low over the guilty dog.

'And just what do you think you're doing, little lady?' Lisa would ask, before promptly ejecting Fizz Dog back on to the floor and the comfort of the numerous dog beds we had laid out for her around the house. Dog beds that were obviously not up to her Rottweiler high standards.

We had known that getting our former Afghan strays to respect their surroundings would present our first big challenge. House-training a pair of dogs that had basically lived a feral existence in one of the harshest environments on the planet wasn't going to be easy. In fact, a part of me already suspected it might be just a tad impossible.

Our task hadn't exactly been helped by the fact the pair of them had been treated so well in quarantine. The kennel girls, especially Rebecca and Vicky – two 20-somethings who adored dogs and loved their job – had felt so sorry for the two Afghan refugees that they had made the dogs' six-month confinement more comfortable by giving each dog its own armchair to relax in and watch the world go by. Telling them that our new, nicely upholstered furniture was out of bounds was going to be a tough ask after that.

Much as we wanted them to behave like well-trained, westernised dogs, we realised we had to be realistic and cut them some slack. It was easy to forget sometimes that these were dogs from another world, one in which the trappings of modern life – as we know it – simply didn't exist.

Although Lisa acted like Tali was a constant thorn in her side, I knew deep down that Tali – even with all her erratic ways – was definitely becoming Lisa's dog. Quite early on, I had caught Lisa spending time cuddling the little nightmare. Tali would sit next to Lisa (always with one back leg oddly stuck straight up in the air), waiting for the fuss and attention she knew was coming her way. And for some reason I couldn't fathom, Lisa had taken to calling Tali by a new name, Banagebear. Where that had come from I had no idea.

Tali's sticking-up-leg habit underlined the fact that we knew so little about the two dogs' backgrounds.

I was aware of some of what had happened to them before they had come to live with us, but who knew what had happened before I had taken them in? How many fights had Nowzad been forced to take part in? How many litters of pups had Tali had to undergo?

It didn't bear thinking about.

All I knew about Nowzad's early years was that he'd probably been selected and raised specifically for dog-fighting. While based in Now Zad, I had come across other dogs that had been selected and trained for this purpose and the treatment they received was appalling. All of them had had their tails and ears crudely snipped off so that their opponent had nothing to get a grip on during a fight. I had seen fighting dogs tied to walls by thin, almost razor-like wire round their necks. It had been as if we were on another planet, the culture completely alien to us.

Beyond this, however, I knew nothing. I reckoned he was five or six years old, but that was pure guesswork. He could have been nine or ten. But either way you looked at it, Nowzad had had a hard paper-round, that was for sure. He was still a fine, proud-looking animal, though. His tan-coloured hair more or less covered his entire body, except for a little whitish grey around the muzzle, and a tuft of short white hair sticking out of either cropped ear. His eyes were oddly dark and seemed to stare right through you if he was scared or alert. I knew that we had to take our time with him, get to know his ways and his personality.

One of the first things we'd learned was how to judge his mood. The easiest way to do this was to watch what he did with his short docked tail. Upright wagging meant he was excited. Straight up in the air with no wagging meant watch out, because he wasn't happy about something. Short stump tight against his backside meant he was scared.

It was his scared look that concerned me the most as I sensed I knew what it meant. Although he could come across at times as a ferocious animal, deep down Nowzad was really just a confused and extremely frightened dog. The aggression was just a means of defending himself from everything he didn't understand. Which were most things, at the moment.

In this sense he was no different to many dogs here in the UK. We have more than our fair share of misunderstood dogs, too, many of which are put to sleep without a second thought for just looking aggressive, let alone due to actually attacking anybody. Besides which, nearly 99 per cent of the time it is the human influence on the dog that has caused the problems: the dogs are not given the chance to prove otherwise.

Woe betide us if we were ever as strict on some of the humans walking our streets as we were with our dog population.

In particular, I understood why Nowzad was wary of other dogs. He was simply a product of his surroundings and the treatment he had received. And having spent time living in those surroundings, I knew that he would have had it tough. Whether he was scavenging for food or being forced into a dogfight, as far as he was concerned all other dogs were potential trouble. And his policy was to attack first and not bother with the questions till afterwards.

I knew what Nowzad was capable of and I really believed he could fit into a normal way of life. It was going to be a long, slow road though, of that I was certain. Nowzad had spent his entire adult life, so far, as an untrained fighting stray, with no perception of what it was like to live within a loving home. But we would get there – eventually.

The daunting task we now faced was to reverse all those years of conditioning.

Trying to adapt two Afghan dogs to life in the west might have been a nightmare, but at least it was a nightmare that kept me active. Everything else about our lives now seemed to involve paperwork.

To channel the fund-raising efforts to get Nowzad and Tali flown to the UK the year before, Lisa and I had, almost without thinking about it, formed a charity called Nowzad Dogs.

The beginnings of it had started whilst I was still serving out in Helmand. My mum had arranged some publicity in the local press back in East Anglia regarding the then unknown future that Nowzad and Tali would possibly have.

Out of nowhere, I had started receiving letters and cheques from people all over the country wanting to help the two Afghan strays find a 'for ever' home. Jena had been adopted by the founder of the Afghan rescue, a rescue centre that Lisa had luckily found on the internet and which had been set up with assistance by a charity called Mayhew International and a determined aid worker from America called Pam in 2003. Jena (or Mocha as we discovered she was now called), was enjoying life living near to the ocean along the eastern coast of America.

But that is where the happy endings stopped. I had placed five adult dogs into what I had assumed was the safety of the waiting taxi as Kilo Company were hours away from being rotated out of the Now Zad compound. Without explanation only three of the adult dogs had made it. To this day I still do not know what happened to RPG and AK. Maybe they escaped from a left-open door when the vehicle stopped? We just don't know and never will. I try not to think about it. It hurts if I do.

But by the time I had returned to the UK, the support for Nowzad and Tali was snowballing. The cheques were getting more frequent, and also more substantial. And they always came with the same message: '*Please continue to do something for the strays of Afghanistan.*'

On setting up the charity, Lisa and I had agreed that we wanted to do some good in the world, and even if we made a difference to just one dog by finding it a loving home, we were going in the right direction, we reckoned.

Our long-term plan and more meaningful role of promoting animal welfare in Afghanistan could be tackled when we had the backing and funds behind us to do so.

As senior physical-training instructors in the military, neither Lisa nor I knew anything about running a charity, and had naively assumed the job and the associated paper-work would be child's play. We also assumed it would be a small-scale thing that wouldn't really catch on.

How wrong could we have been?

The story of what we'd done in bringing the dogs back to the UK had become national news. We'd been on the BBC and appeared in newspapers like the *Mail on Sunday*. We'd known that Britain was a nation of animal lovers but we'd been taken completely by surprise. Suddenly, we became the only source of information about the strays of Afghanistan and the bleak future they faced. And for soldiers who found themselves bonding with an Afghan stray, we became their only chance of hope.

We had bribed and cajoled several friends and supporters into taking on the role of trustees to get the charity going, but they, too, had busy, full-time jobs, so we felt reluctant to pile yet more work on top of them. Slowly but surely, the charity was beginning to take over any remaining free time we had in our day.

The arrival of the charity mail had now become a major event. For a while I had found it funny to shout 'Incoming!' as I threw the latest bag full of charity mail on the table in front of Lisa. But as news of Nowzad and Tali and their new lives spread, we noticed the 'incoming' mail sack was turning up more and more often.

We soon began to realise that there was no manual on how to run a charity, and at times it felt like we were in a paperwork minefield with no idea which way to tread. There was the website to update, thank-you letters to write and post, a supporter database to maintain, donation and banking paperwork to keep on top of and, of course, the planning for any dog rescue we were asked to assist with. It began to seem never-ending, but we didn't mind. It was a novelty and it felt good to be doing something positive in what most saw as a lost cause of a country.

As ever, though, it didn't take much to remind me of why I was doing this. My climbing equipment was dumped in the corner alongside me, on top of a pile of newspaper cuttings. I could make out the headlines on the top one. It was about Nowzad and his arrival here in the UK.

I clicked on the photo files on our computer and found a picture of one of Tali's pups crammed tightly into the metal crate we had used for their long journey to the Afghan Animal Shelter. The screen was filled with an image of the pup, its head poking through the wire mesh of the crate.

At the time, we had assumed that losing the two adult dogs had been the worst that was going to happen. But, as if to prove how dangerous Afghanistan was in every conceivable way, the centre had then been hit by a lethal outbreak of parvovirus.

Until I had received the email detailing the bad news, I had never heard of the disease. But it was a nasty piece of work as far as diseases go and killed all but one of the pups: only one skinny, runt-like pup from Tali's litter, a dog we decided to call Helmand, had survived.

I clicked the computer mouse to find some more recent photographs. One was of a scrawny, frightened-looking young dog, still in the Afghan rescue centre. It was Helmand and, thanks to the growing popularity of the charity, I now knew he was coming 'home', if you could call six months of quarantine 'home' at the end of January 2008. The little pup had touched the heart of our supporters and I guessed that for a lot of people, he was the last piece of the puzzle that made up the story of the Now Zad pack. They'd been generous in their donations and we'd now finally got together the necessary funds to arrange a flight back to the UK and six months in a quarantine facility.

There were times when I looked at Tali and the feelings of guilt at not saving her pups could still flood in with the speed of an early spring tide. But at least now I knew that one of them was about to have a better life.

In the meantime, my proper day-time job was proving to be as far removed from my previous Royal Marine life as I could imagine, and not in a good way, either.

On the face of it, the recent promotion had been good news. The not-quite-so-good news was that promotion had come with a desk attached, something I'd not exactly thought too much about. As I settled into the new role, I was amazed at how tiring it felt flying a desk.

My previous job on return from Afghanistan had been as a physical-training instructor for a commando unit. It had kept me active all day. I would either spend my hours leading a physical-training session for the lads or leading a group out on the moors. That had been just the way I liked it. Limiting the amount of time I had spent behind my desk was the number one priority for me, but my new life was quite the opposite.

When I say it was a desk job that was only a guess: I could barely see the desk beneath the pile of folders that I had found on it when I had first arrived.

The handover from the guy who'd been there before me was simple: 'Colour Sergeant Farthing, your job is to organise outdoor adventure activities for the 7,000 or so marines and attached units of the Commando Brigade, preferably activities overseas and somewhere hot, to break up the stress of their operational tours in Afghanistan and Iraq.'

My predecessor had briefed me as quickly as he could, packing his stuff up as he spoke, strangely keen to get out of the office.

'Okay, no problem,' I had thought. Organising activity trips for the lads was something I had done as part of my last unit. And I knew the value of such trips in helping lads get over the often traumatic experience of six months on the frontline. This would simply be the same sort of thing but on a grander scale, and with a grander budget.

Or so I had thought. My preconceptions on that were quickly corrected: 'Oh, and by the way, I forgot to mention that you only have £40,000 to do it with,' the departing colour sergeant had yelled over his shoulder as he left the office for the last time.

My old maths teacher, who had never had much faith in me, would have been proud as I quickly calculated that it couldn't be done. Just to confirm what I already knew, a few quick taps on the keys of the desk calculator revealed I would have the princely sum of precisely £5.71 to spend on each marine.

'How the hell am I supposed to do this?' I had called down the hall after him.

The silence was deafening. He was long gone.

After much head scratching – and the occasional banging of my head on the piles of paperwork covering the desk – I had got stuck in.

I was soon learning some of the rules of office life. For instance, I already understood the law that meant the moment I finished one task, the phone would ring with another one that had to be completed by yesterday. The new task would also deplete further my already limited funds, usually scuppering my plans to spend it on something else as well.

The politics of the job were soon wearing me down, too. While one aspect of my work was to help relieve the stress that a lot of my colleagues experienced on their return from active service, ironically achieving this did very little for my own stress levels.

Throughout my career the emphasis had been on winning the fight against an enemy, no matter who they were. Here, there was no enemy – not in the traditional sense, anyway. Now with little more than a few hours' handover, I was committed to working at a desk. In Afghanistan what we did was second nature, but behind a desk I was a fish out of water, and I was starting to understand how Nowzad must feel – so far away from a lifestyle he understood and out of his comfort zone – more and more, if anything Nowzad was used to hardships and being the top dog. Now suddenly he was part of a pack and food appeared as if by magic twice a day. I could understand his confusion at times. Maybe Nowzad was always on edge waiting for the moment he would be thrown back into the thick of it.

No matter how much I tried to remain calm, explaining to some faceless officer on the other end of a phone why I needed extra money to send our lads scuba diving was a real challenge. A challenge that I seemed to be failing at, constantly.

No matter how much proof I produced that arduous adventurous activities helped heal the mental scars of post-traumatic stress, I got nothing in response. I was soon convinced that everyone higher up the food chain was more interested in keeping within their budgets and not rocking the boat. More than once I was told to get back in my box; one officer told me in no uncertain terms that my pay scale didn't allow me to comment.

It wasn't long before the frustration was beginning to show itself to my colleagues. 'Fighting the frigging Taliban in Afghanistan is easier than dealing with this lot,' I muttered under my breath one morning as I slammed the phone down yet again, after a disturbingly one-sided conversation with a senior officer. In a condescending voice he had informed me that none of our troops were suffering from PTSD.

I knew the guy had never been on the frontline in Helmand. He had no idea what the reality was.

'Touchy touchy,' a voice had called over from behind a large computer monitor on the other side of the room.

'Bugger off, Andy, I am dealing with idiots here,' I replied, the pent-up anger booming round the office walls.

I had known Andy, a Royal Marine Warrant Officer, since we'd both been corporals serving at the Royal Marines' base in Kent. With a civilian colleague called Kevin, he now ran the Royal Marines Sports Association from the same office as me.

Andy had been in the office longer than I had so had arranged it the way he liked it. The main feature was the world's biggest fish tank. Apparently Andy's wife had made him relocate it to work because the fish were taking over her house.

I could see her point. The tank was so huge I could have swum in the thing. Where Andy had actually kept it at home I had no idea. In a funny way, however, it added something to the atmosphere in the office.

Inside the tank, Andy's collection of multicoloured,

exotic fish would swim in unison one way and then dart left or right together, as if being drilled by a regimental sergeant major on the parade square. I had found that watching the fish had a really calming influence on me and proved quite soothing in times of stress.

Which is another way of saying I stared at them quite a lot as I continually re-evaluated how I had ended up behind a mountain of paperwork. I hadn't joined the Royal Marines to become desk-bound.

And as if the office politics and my annoyance at the lack of support I was getting weren't bad enough, I discovered that the job also had the potential to land me in hot water with Lisa.

One evening, I had arrived home feeling a bit more positive about things, having talked to some lads who'd been on one of the few projects I had managed successfully to organise during my early days at the job: a skydiving expedition to Florida.

'I saw the lads' pictures from the skydiving,' I had said to Lisa as I came through the door. She was in the process of hoovering and cleaning the house, having only got in from work herself five minutes before me.

'What were they like?' she asked without stopping, as she simultaneously lifted the coffee table with one hand while working the vacuum cleaner expertly under it with the other.

'Well cool,' I said, mimicking raising my hands in the air while pretending to fall through the sky. 'Wish I had gone now – the pool party with all the Yank girls looked hoofing.'

The house suddenly became unnervingly quiet as the noisy sucking of the vacuum cleaner died with a stern flick of Lisa's finger.

'Oh, shit,' I thought to myself.

With the vacuum cleaner still in hand, Lisa's head turned to look menacingly at me.

'I wish I had gone for the sky diving, honey, the sky diving,' I said with as much sincerity as I could muster.

Lisa continued to stare deep into my soul with the eyes of a woman scorned.

'I mean I wouldn't have gone to the parties,' I back-pedalled frantically. But it was no good. Lisa just fixed me with her 'Yet another wrong answer' look.

I started to back out of the living-room door, almost falling over the parked form of Tali as I did so.

'I would just have applied all the suntan cream,' I said, skilfully ducking the thrown cushion, which having missed my head by millimetres went on to hit the kitchen wall behind me and crash-land in the washing-up bowl.

'I'll make some tea,' I announced from the safety of the kitchen, as the vacuum cleaner whirred back into life.

What really depressed me the most, however, was that the workload in the office made it really hard to find time for looking after the dogs.

Our new home was close enough to the base for me to

be able to make a mad dash home at lunchtimes to give them a run, but otherwise they were left to their own devices during the daytime hours. Strangely, though, with their Afghan blood still strong, Nowzad and Tali were, in fact, quite happy to chill out all day. In fact, I had a feeling that at times they were a tad annoyed that their siestas were interrupted by my arrival home.

Fizz Dog and Beamer Boy, on the other hand, made me feel guilty about not taking them out so much. Together, they had spent their lives running around like idiots with me wherever I ended up going, but were now confined to only enjoying our early morning and evening walks.

In years gone by, I had also been allowed to take the pair of them on to the base with me, but for the first time in my military career, I had not been allowed to take them into work with the new job.

It only added to the sense of how different our lives had suddenly become.

CHAPTER FOUR

24/7

The early-morning sun was just about visible in the eastern sky, but in actuality it really needn't have bothered making the effort. Our back garden was frozen solid as was to be expected during the first few days of February, the grass covered in a thin sheen of frost and, as I opened the back door, the cold air rushed in like a hurricane. Still, every cloud has a silver lining, I thought – at least the glittering, frozen dog crap dotted round the back garden would be easier to pick up, which was just as well, as owning four dogs meant on occasions there was a lot of it to pick up.

Collecting the dog crap had become something of an art form for me. I was an expert on how to retrieve the stuff easily and how to dispose of it. For instance, I had noticed that, of late, the supermarkets were, for some reason, putting lots more tiny circular holes in the carrier bags we packed the weekly shop into. More than once I had been caught out as I had used one of the bags to scoop up dog poo.

'Bastards,' I had tutted as I looked at my contaminated hand with disgust.

I had also learned a fair bit about the dogs' other bodily functions. But there, too, I still had practical problems.

This morning, as was now the norm, I turned to the dogs who were all sitting eagerly in the kitchen, waiting to be let out. Happily, Nowzad was amongst them, as he had been living full-time in the house for just over a month now. It had taken a lot of effort, but he had finally learnt to use the outdoor facilities.

He was, however, still getting used to some of the other finer points of living in a western house. With the weather not suited to drying our washing on the line outside, we had been forced to use the plastic drying racks that attached to the front of our radiators. A few mornings ago I had come downstairs to find Nowzad snuggled up in a pile of Lisa's underwear that he had carefully taken the time to carry to his bed.

'Nice going, buddy,' I had said to him as he had lifted his head, his sleepy eyes startled as I snapped a thong out from under his front paw. 'I didn't bring back a cross-dressing Afghan hound, did I?' I asked him as I held up the shredded garment. 'Ohh, you are so in trouble when Mrs F comes down, dude.' I smiled as I rubbed his head and retrieved the other five items of underwear that he had stolen.

All had been used as chew toys.

That episode had taught us not to leave things we valued within Nowzad's reach now that he lived indoors, but at least I didn't have to spend hours on my hands and knees scrubbing the side of the sofa any more.

Now I yanked the back door more widely open and yelled, 'Wee time!'

Beamer Boy and Fizz Dog had no problems with the cold so both dogs shot out of the door, harrowingly close to stampeding over my slipper-covered feet. Fizz Dog was barking as usual as she chased Beamer Boy out into the crisp morning.

Nowzad and Tali were a different matter. They reluctantly eased themselves out of bed, but lasted outdoors for about five seconds before turning and bolting for the warmth of the living room.

'Every bloody time,' I sighed.

It really was the same every morning. For two dogs that had survived in the barren wastes of several freezing Afghan winters, they had definitely got a little too used to their home comforts. Getting them outside for an early-morning wee was becoming a nightmare. I had a feeling both dogs would lie in their pits until midday if they were given the chance.

That wasn't going to happen, however. I couldn't have the pair of them turning to fat. Nowzad, in particular, would easily put too much weight on if we weren't careful about making sure he ate and exercised correctly. He was slightly lame in his right rear leg, maybe due to an injury, so I didn't want him adding to any problems in later life by becoming unfit now.

I let them know my thoughts in no uncertain terms. 'You two get back here NOW,' I shouted, in a voice that normally had 30-odd marines leaping to do my bidding. From the lack of response I got, I knew they weren't shifting without another fight.

I glanced at my watch. I was going to be late for work if I wasn't careful.

The fight to get them outside was only the start of an average morning's conflicts. Once that was out of the way, I still had to give all four of them a walk and, last but not least, endure the battle that was feeding time.

It was a pain in the arse operation to be honest. In many ways it was no better than it had been in Afghanistan when I'd had a daily struggle to keep order whilst feeding my pack of feral dogs.

More than once my mind had flashed back to that time. My problems had begun when I'd just had two dogs, Nowzad and the lively little RPG. Naively I had assumed that I could simply feed the pair using the two stainless steel bowls I had 'borrowed' from the Afghan Police. I'd fill the bowls up, leave them to it and get on with all the other stuff I was supposed to be doing while I was moonlighting as a dog warden. Wrong.

I could still picture the mayhem that was the first feeding time.

Nowzad had scoffed his food down like it was his first proper meal ever. Which it may well have been, of course. While he had been devouring the leftover rations, RPG had steadily sniffed and munched away at his meal. Content in the knowledge that they were both all right, I had turned my back, a very naive mistake as it proved.

Having successfully emptied his bowl Nowzad had immediately looked for some more food. He had leapt at the still-eating RPG determined to drive him away to eat his food as well. That was probably the way it always was in his world. Survival of the fiercest was the order of the day. It had only been by placing a combat boot in Nowzad's midriff that I had managed to end Nowzad's ferocious assault on the skinnier and terrified RPG.

From then on I had been forced to watch them like a hawk at feeding times. Every meal time I had to remind Nowzad that once he had eaten his food he was to sit patiently until RPG had finished. My only concession was that at the end the pair could lick each other's already immaculately licked-clean bowls. Just to be sure there was nothing left.

Nowzad was more or less the same now.

He wanted to eat first. I was willing to accommodate this, and luckily the other dogs toed the line. Tali was more laid back about her eating than Nowzad, and Fizz Dog and Beamer Boy knew the score: they knew they'd get fed eventually. They had learned to wait patiently until the new arrivals finished.

Unfortunately, Nowzad still had his Oliver Twist habit. As soon as he had licked his bowl clean, he would set off with the intention of snatching any remaining food from the other three bowls. So from the start, Lisa and I had to spend time sitting by his side, overseeing his behaviour and trying to train him out of it during the twice-daily feeding.

And so it was again this morning. I began by first making Nowzad sit and wait before placing his bowl down. As usual he lurched at it before it had hit the ground, forcing me to remove it. Sometimes, numerous false starts later, I would first have to release him from the mini-headlock I'd been forced to put him in to get the message through.

The instant I'd done so he'd dive into his bowl to scoff the dried chicken and rice dog food, which had become his favourite. Why it was his favourite, I don't know. After a few beers one night, I had tried it and failed to see the appeal.

With Nowzad fed, my job then was to keep him under control so that he wouldn't venture after more food.

'Nowzad, no,' I kept repeating as the others tucked into their breakfast.

'Nowzad, sit,' I would say countless times before the Afghan nightmare reluctantly squatted back into a sitting position. 'Now wait, you poor starving dog.'

Once they were all finished, it was like musical chairs as all four dogs frantically tried to lick all the bowls, looking for the last missed morsel before the music stopped and the bowls were taken away.

As usual, all this took time, precious time. But as the weeks started to slip quickly by, I could see some small improvements. Nowzad was slowly getting the message: for a start, I didn't have to put him in a headlock so many times.

Timewise, though, this morning's antics were no exception to the norm. The whole palaver of getting them to have a wee, walking and feeding them took up more than an hour. It wasn't an hour I could afford to lose. I was definitely going to be late for work.

Not content with taking up most of our free time, seven months after we had started it, the charity had begun taking over the house.

The smaller spare bedroom had been the first to succumb as it had been converted into our charity HQ. The computer had been stuck in there too, as had all the files, and printed material that we were now churning out. But when the room had become clogged up with the mountains of paper, it had begun to spill over into other parts of the house.

It was only when one of my mates, Mally, came down to stay that it suddenly dawned on us how the charity had staged a bloodless coup and taken over complete control of our home. By now the main guest room was full of cardboard boxes containing the charity's promotional flyers and posters. There was a bed in there somewhere but as Lisa and I set about getting the room ready for him, it had been hard to pinpoint its exact location.

'This is bloody stupid,' Lisa said as we both stared into

what looked like an office stationery storeroom. 'This is a guest room without room for a guest.'

'Mally won't mind sleeping on the floor,' I replied, which was true. Mally had been my best man and, of course, he was a marine. 'And anyway, we'll probably be three sheets to the wind by bedtime,' I tried to add helpfully. Mally did like his red wine.

'I'm not bothered about Mally,' Lisa said, shaking her head. I reckoned she still remembered his best man speech. 'I mean,' she said, pausing to continue surveying the scene, 'where has our house gone?'

She had a point.

The charity had finally claimed the last available room of the house. But as I looked down the stairs at Tali staring back up at me through the bars of the kid's stair gate we'd installed to keep the dogs downstairs, I was reminded of why we'd handed the house over.

Our number one aim was to help those soldiers that found themselves in the same position in which I had been; those who'd found a dog and wanted to adopt them and bring them back to the UK (or who, rather, as was more often the case, had been found by a dog and adopted). And whenever I got an email from a soldier asking for help, I really didn't care about the state of the house. But I could spend the rest of my life bringing thousands of Afghan dogs to the UK but I would never solve the underlying problem. We wanted to promote animal welfare in a country currently devoid of any notion of it. The next step would be to start a neutering programme, but that was possibly getting well ahead of myself at the moment.

And anyway who cared if the house was currently used for charity storage? Not many people visited us anyway, I reasoned. We had dogs.

The screen seemed to fade in and out of focus as I sat at the computer, staring at the inbox that had filled to overflowing in the nine hours or so since I had left home for work this morning.

The good news was that it contained nothing of high importance. The bad news was that there were still lots of emails that needed replies and I was knackered at the end of another draining day at the office.

'I've just spent all day at work on the military computer,' I said to myself as I continued to delete spam and mark the emails that needed a reply. It seemed as though my life was now nothing but work, 24/7.

Of course, I had no one to blame but myself. It had been my choice to start the charity. I just wished we had factored in the need for an administration assistant.

I was also becoming weary of the reaction we were sometimes receiving via email or when we were out and about. People's reaction varied considerably when I told them what we were doing. Most were supportive and enthusiastic. Some, however, doubted my sanity. 'Are you mad?' they'd ask. 'Animal welfare in *Afghanistan*?'

Others, however, were more critical. 'What about the

kids out there?' was the most common comment. 'How can you not do anything for the kids but spend your time looking after *dogs*?'

I would usually stand there and stare at them, often trying to decide whether a punch was the best answer. Common sense, thankfully, always prevailed, and I would explain patiently that I couldn't just walk down an alleyway in Afghanistan, pick up a dirt-covered, starving little boy or girl, like some rock star on a personal crusade, and say: 'Come on, little one, you're coming home to the UK with me.' I had to operate in the real world. And that world was a hard one, with tough choices.

Some people didn't buy this argument, so I would simply ask them what they were doing for Afghanistan. Their failure to reply said it all.

I had fought in Afghanistan. Others like me still continue the fight against the Taliban, protecting and providing for the children of Afghanistan as they do so. If the Taliban were allowed back into power then the Afghan kids of tomorrow would have nothing: no education, no welfare, no music, nothing. No freedom at all. Hell, all men of a certain age would have to grow a beard. Even 'American-style haircuts' were banned (whatever an American-style haircut was). Anybody deemed sporting that particular style would be whisked off to visit the Religious Police barber and in the past had been punished by being forced to pay for the haircut.

Women would fare no better: they'd be confined to the house to bring up the children and covered from head to toe if they were allowed to venture outside. Even if a male visitor was invited into the home he would never be allowed in the same room as the women of the house. A woman's life, under the Taliban, was one of isolation and subservience.

And then there was the severity of the punishments meted out by the ruling Taliban. Flogging, stoning, amputation and hanging were common sights during their time in power.

And most young Afghans would be brought up to detest the western non-believers with a passion that few who had not been to Afghanistan could begin to imagine.

But with knowledge comes power: give the young men and women of Afghanistan a voice and a chance at a future, and the Taliban would be in trouble.

As a charity, that was way outside our remit. We couldn't do that. But I took comfort from the fact that at least as a charity we were attempting to do something positive. By promoting animal welfare through proper stray-dog population control, for instance, we would be helping rid Afghanistan of the deadliest of diseases that affects both dogs and humans – rabies, and maybe, just maybe, we could stop dogs being born into a world of starvation and cruel, short lives.

We also hoped that if we could teach even the most basic of animal-welfare techniques to the outlying villages and farms, then they in turn would be better equipped to look after their mules and goats, which are the lifeblood of all the remote communities.

But explaining all of that to some random person who assumed we could just walk up to the kids in Afghanistan and make their lives better was at best annoying. I had no intention of being lectured to by some uninformed busybody who wasn't making any valuable contribution to anything but their own welfare.

Besides I was enjoying what we were attempting to do. It had a good feel about it.

'Er, Pen, a little help might be good,' the anxious voice called from the living room.

I ignored it and finished opening the two beers in the kitchen.

'Are you two not friends yet?' I asked a few seconds later as I returned to the living room to be greeted by a familiar sight.

Cavey, a civilian mate with whom I often went canoeing, was standing nervously with his back against the wall as Nowzad sat rigidly to attention, eyeballing him.

'Just ignore him, mate, he isn't going to hurt you,' I said as I handed over the open bottle of beer.

'He's still staring at me,' Cavey said, reaching for the drink without taking his eyes off Nowzad.

'I wasn't talking to you; I was talking to the dog.' I chuckled as I stroked the top of Nowzad's head with my free hand.

I knew it was safe to have some fun with the situation. Nowzad was incapable of doing anything nasty at the moment, even if he had wanted to. With his tan-coloured plastic muzzle fitted securely to his head, he looked like a canine version of Hannibal Lecter. But beyond making a really scary growling noise, that was the extent of his threat.

Despite this, I could see Cavey wasn't totally happy with the situation so I tried to help.

'Nowzad, he's your friend. Let him sit down, please, buddy. I know he smells funny.'

'Ho ho ho,' Cavey laughed weakly as he watched Nowzad trot off. He then peeled himself off the wall, taking a large gulp of beer as he did so.

This behaviour wasn't anything new. In fact, I could have bet a million dollars that this was going to happen the moment we got the phone call from Cavey saying he was in the area and needed somewhere to stay for the night.

Cavey was a really good mate. I had first met him ten years earlier on a canoeing course at the National Outdoor Centre in Wales, although it had been in the bar over a few beers after an extreme day of paddling down gnarly rivers that we had begun to chat. We had been the only two propping up the deserted bar so the choice of drinking companions had been limited: the lightweights that made up the rest of our course had sacked it early and gone to bed. (Which, with hindsight, had probably been the best option as both me and Cavey awoke the following morning with banging heads but, thankfully, and as always, the first dunking of the day sorted us out a treat).

Cavey had the same sense of humour as most marines and was a very handy guy to have around when I was upside down on a swollen river which, with my paddling skills, was most of the time.

Tall and lanky, Cavey was also older than me, which I always said was pretty obvious when we stood side by side. We were great friends despite him being a civilian, and as I reckoned I would be too one day, I had decided it would be prudent to extend my circle of friends to include a few who didn't spend their days camouflaged in bushes.

In his formative years Cavey had worked as a train driver, which had completely thrown me when I had found out. I couldn't say I had been overly stoked at being a passenger in his van, let alone imagining sitting on a train capable of 120 miles an hour knowing he was at the helm.

Cavey had visited us before since the Afghan dogs had arrived, and it had been quite obvious that Nowzad didn't like him. Which was why I had taken the precaution this time of putting the muzzle on him: I didn't want to take a chance. Nowzad didn't like the muzzle, of course, but he had no choice in the matter. Not unless we all wanted to risk ending up in the local A & E.

We had tried to defuse the situation by introducing the two of them to each other outside, but it hadn't worked. Every time the same scenario played out: Cavey would come into the house and Nowzad would immediately try and have a go at him. To be fair to Nowzad, it wasn't rabid, snarling aggression; it was more like grumpy growling followed by a lunge and nip. Except Nowzad sported some gnarly big teeth (around the obvious gaps), so I wasn't sure his nip would be just a nip.

Not that it was me he was trying to eat.

Cavey was a regular part of our life so we had tried everything we could think of to solve the problem. We'd actually been quite imaginative about it. We had tried accidentally 'bumping' into Cavey whilst on a walk round the block, but it hadn't worked. We had tried getting Cavey to arrive at the back door laden with smelly dog treats, but that hadn't worked. We then tried him arriving at the front door just in case this made a difference, but that hadn't worked either. Finally, we had smuggled Cavey into the house so he was already part of the furniture when Nowzad arrived back from a walk. But, nope, that didn't get us anywhere, either: it was if Nowzad could smell him as we rounded the corner that led to our house.

Instead, we coached Cavey to ignore Nowzad for 30 minutes or so while we attempted to chat. He did his best to pretend there wasn't a grumpy old dog squaring up to him in the corner of the room, but it wasn't much fun for him.

In another change of tack one day, I stroked and played with Nowzad while attempting to chat to Cavey who was standing at the far end of the back garden. But with the same result. There was just no getting away from the fact: Nowzad just wanted to eat Cavey.

'Nowzad, leave him alone. You have no idea where he's been,' I would say.

The consolation was that Cavey didn't mind that much. He was fully aware of what Nowzad had been through and was more than happy to work through our plans to socialise Nowzad. We'd come to see it as the marker. If Nowzad accepted Cavey into the house then our work was done. Which was why today was annoying. Despite having done everything we'd asked him to do in order to bond with our Afghan arrival, Cavey still wasn't on Nowzad's Christmas card list.

The only other people Nowzad would see on a semi-regular basis were my in-laws. For some reason, the daft dog didn't bat an eyelid with them. No muzzle, no restraint needed. He just didn't seem to care that they were in the house one little bit. Brian and Marlene would even ruffle his head and Nowzad would be quite content to sit there and soak up the attention. Nowzad was one odd dog.

We had no idea what it was about Cavey.

Now, as I held Nowzad's collar, Cavey made his way over to the sofa. 'Look, buddy, how many times are we going to go through this?' I whispered into Nowzad's ear. 'He's one of the good guys, so leave him alone.'

Cavey sat down on the sofa and was immediately mobbed by Fizz Dog, Beamer Boy and Tali, all wanting attention.

I let Nowzad go, just for him to spin on the spot searching for his nemesis. He immediately clocked where Cavey had gone to, and streaked over to square up to him once more.

'I give up,' I said as I plonked myself down next to Cavey,

who by now had discarded his beer on the coffee table so he could use both hands to stroke all three dogs.

Nowzad didn't try to bite Cavey but inched closer to set about sniffing his jeans through the plastic muzzle.

'Have you been rolling around in shit again?' I asked Cavey, as Nowzad sniffed intently up and down his right leg.

CHAPTER FIVE

F*U*B*A*R

M y feet were well and truly cemented to the floor as I sat on the sofa with the laptop across my knees. The curled-up figure of Nowzad lying across my feet saw to that.

No matter where I went in the house, Nowzad would push himself up, his rear legs seeming to struggle until he was standing, and then trot after me. The instant I stood or sat still for 30 seconds, he would gently drop himself to the ground next to my feet and curl up in a ball.

I had tried a few times to pre-empt this by asking him to stay put: 'Nowzad, I am just going to make a cup of tea. Stay there and I'll be back in three minutes.' But no sooner had I stood up, my loyal buddy would make a small groaning sound, haul himself up into a standing position and paddle his way after me. 'Nowzie,' I would say, shaking my head in what I hoped was a discouraging way. But it didn't work. He stuck to me like glue, as if the thought of me leaving him behind again was too hard to handle.

For a brief moment, I would think about our first encounters back in Helmand. I remembered how I had been surprised, and touched, by the warmth that this ferocious-looking animal had shown me once we'd established a bond of trust between us.

This was why the email that had just popped into my inbox immediately caught my eye. The subject read simply: Afghan dog needs help.

I opened up the email immediately and began scrolling through the long and detailed message.

It wasn't the most straightforward communication, it had to be said. From what I could make out it was from a Dutch lady called Nathalie, who was somehow connected with a Romanian dog rescue organisation. At first I couldn't see the connection with Afghanistan. But then she explained that she was writing on behalf of a Dutch marine who had adopted an Afghan stray and was desperate to give it a home in the Netherlands. But he was facing the same problems as I had encountered: the military would not help, and he had no idea of any rescue centre that existed.

'Sounds like a job for us,' I said, with a wink at Nowzad.

I had to chuckle when I read the name of the dog concerned. She was called Fubar. 'I bet Nathalie has no idea what that means,' I said to myself. But I did.

As a kid I had been fascinated by everything to do with the Vietnam War, for all the wrong reasons, I guess. The image of a helicopter gunship circling over heavy jungle had somehow captured my imagination.

I had been introduced to the acronym 'FUBAR' in the pages of a great book about the conflict, *Chicken Hawk*, the story of a US helicopter pilot during his tour of Vietnam. FUBAR was an American acronym for when things got really nasty during war. As they often did.

'FUBAR,' I said out loud to Nowzad at my feet, 'Fucked Up Beyond All Recognition. How could they name their dog Fubar?' I was still chuckling several minutes later as I began what I hoped would be the rescue operation for her.

It took several emails to piece together the story of Fubar and I quickly saw why she had come to mean so much to her rescuers. One of the photos I was sent showed a happy-go-lucky bundle of mainly white fluff trotting round with her tail in the air amid the HESCO blocks, erected as protection from incoming mortars in the Dutch soldiers' camp.

She was a distinctive-looking dog, of that there was no doubt. With dark streaks of black that ran round each eye and ear on either side of her head, on an almost perfectly white body, she reminded me of a caped crusader super-hero from a Marvel comic.

It turned out that she had been minutes from death when she had been plucked from danger by the Dutch marine, Chris, with whom I was eventually put in email contact. Chris had been part of a six-man detachment of Dutch marines that had been stationed in a patrol base north of Tarin Kowt in the Uruzgan region of central Afghanistan. They were mentoring a 40-strong company from a recently formed division of the Afghan National Army, which would have been a tough and demanding job if the ANA stationed with us had been anything to go by.

The patrol base had been tasked with a search and clear operation through a particularly thickly wooded area known as 'the Green'. Their mission had been simple: to seek out a Taliban improvised explosive device (IED) enabler.

I had experienced drives around the mine-and-IED-littered Afghan landscape during my tour of duty, and Chris's description of the operation had been easy for me to picture. He described the low growl of the engines as the only sound around as everyone concentrated on eyeballing every inch of the track in front and to the side of them, quietly dreading what the barren landscape might be hiding.

I remembered that feeling.

Travelling around in an open-top Land Rover with the Afghan winter in full swing, he and his colleagues had worn heavy winter combat clothing to protect themselves from the bitter winter winds.

With about a kilometre to travel before they hit the edge of the Green, where their operation would start in earnest, Chris and his colleagues had watched in horror as the Bushmaster armoured vehicle in front had only narrowly missed a small whitish blob, no bigger than a deflated football, that was curled up just off the edge of the rough track they were driving along.

The underside of the Bushmaster is designed to withstand the blast from a land mine or IED. Its heavy-duty tyres could have crushed the object and the lads inside wouldn't have felt a thing.

However, Chris and the corporal driving the Land Rover had immediately recognised the object for what it was.

'It's a puppy,' Chris's driver had shouted. A very young and freezing puppy.

Chris had exchanged glances with the corporal. He knew what they were both thinking: 'Should we stop?'

But they were part of a large convoy. There was no way on this planet they could stop a major military operation for a puppy.

With no *qualas* – the local name for Afghan farm compounds – anywhere near their current location, the only possible explanation was that the puppy had been abandoned by its mum.

'Maybe the mum dropped it in panic as the convoy approached,' the corporal suggested, as Chris made a split-second decision.

The chances of the puppy surviving the current extreme temperature were pretty remote. In fact, Chris calculated they were probably non-existent.

He ordered his driver to slow down just enough as they drew level with the huddled form of the puppy lying amongst the snow and mud on the edge of the track, only inches from the tyre tracks of the Bushmaster that had just trundled past.

He pushed out from his position behind the machine gun and as his combat boots hit the icy ground, he quickly scooped up the tiny bundle of iced fur before jumping back into the trundling vehicle.

Chris could immediately see that the puppy didn't look good. With one of its tiny eyes seemingly closed through infection, it was shivering violently. Chris had reached into the back of the truck and pulled out an American-style military poncho liner. He arranged it carefully round the puppy like a blanket, and placed the bundle down by his feet, luckily for the pup next to the only working heater in the Land Rover.

The journey into the target area was, thankfully, an uneventful one, but Chris had to weigh up his options. What the hell was he going to do with a one-week-old puppy while they pressed on with their operation and cleared the Green?

The answer came in the form of the heavy-armour mortar vehicles that were going to be positioned on the hillside as over-watch while the ANA and Chris's team breached the objective area.

As they pulled up to the mortar line position, Chris had handed over the wrapped bundle to a surprised gun-line commander with orders to keep the 'little one' warm.

His timing had been spot on. Within minutes both the ANA and the Dutch marines had come under attack from Taliban positions. If the young pup had still been in Chris's care then he would have had no choice but to discard her as he led his lads into action and there would have been no second chance for the abandoned pup.

But Fubar – as Chris had quickly christened the little pup – hadn't been discarded. She had been placed safely inside the heated cab of an armoured vehicle while the gun team laid suppressive fire on to the Taliban positions to support the advancing ANA team.

The operation had been hard and had taken its toll, but Chris had emerged in one piece, with something to look forward to. As he had made his way back to base, he carried the small bundle in the passenger seat of the Land Rover. And, as he was operating out of the patrol base with just six other Dutch marines and a contingent of ANA, he had the chance to look after the fragile little dog without any of the powers-that-be needing to know anything about the abandoned pup. Lady Luck had definitely been on Fubar's side.

There was a strict 'No feral animals' policy at the main Dutch camp. Fubar would have been instantly put to sleep had she been discovered. Instead, she became the focus of everyone's attention at the patrol base.

The moment she had arrived there, Fubar had been gently placed in a hastily constructed bed in a corner of the operations room, which also happened to be the only heated building on the base, and the Dutch medic had been tasked with attempting to clean her bad eye.

It had only been when the tiny pup had settled into a long and deep sleep that the reality of his actions had hit

Chris, and he'd begun to ask himself what the hell he was going to do next.

Again, that was a feeling I could recognise all too well. I had found myself asking that question on an almost daily basis when I had been stuck in Now Zad with a collection of strays and no clue what to do with them.

Nowzad was still lying quietly at my feet as I read the lengthy emails. 'Another one of your buddies being looked after,' I said to him.

The more I read, the more forcefully I was reminded of Nowzad and the other dogs the lads from Kilo Company and I had befriended, and the difference they had made to our day-to-day routine in our isolated compound.

Chris could have been describing our own experience as he wrote: 'Suddenly, from a very operational base, we had a very innocent and friendly little creature with us who was always happy to see us. She made such a difference to our stay.'

That's exactly how we'd felt about Nowzad and the other dogs. They were something to focus our attention on amidst all the danger that surrounded us.

Not everyone was glad to see her, of course. As she had grown, Fubar had begun to venture out and explore the patrol base and her presence hadn't gone down well with the contingent of ANA. Like so many Afghans, they didn't appreciate having an 'unclean' animal wandering around the camp. To protect her, Chris attached her to a long tether tied to the side of the ops room, so that she couldn't stray into trouble.

Fubar's popularity among the Dutch troops was in no doubt, however. The guys in a sniffer-dog detachment at the main Dutch base in Afghanistan, Camp Holland, even used the official resupply chain to forward huge bags of dog food for the little Afghan stray that had stolen the hearts of the Dutch team.

Back in the Netherlands too, awareness about Fubar had grown. The lads on the patrol had written home about their new pal and their families had sent toys and chewie dog bones in the post.

Inevitably, as the end of his tour of duty loomed, Chris's mind had turned to finding a way of getting Fubar out of Afghanistan and home to the Netherlands. His parents had already agreed to take the dog in. It was just a matter of getting him out of Afghanistan.

Just!

Chris had already discovered, as I had, that that was easier said than done. Just like me, he had come up against barrier after barrier. Unlike me, however, he had discovered there was a mechanism for getting dogs out and back to the west: our charity, Nowzad Dogs.

CHAPTER SIX

A Close Shave

'**M**ate, you might want to keep hold of your dog a minute!'

It was little wonder the young guy I was yelling at wasn't responding. As he shuffled along the beach he had his iPod earphones plugged in, his head tucked down low in his thick fur collar and his hands thrust deeply into the pocket of his jeans to protect him from the bitter wind blowing in off the sea.

He was totally oblivious to the fact that his young German Shepherd was charging back and forth at Nowzad, with a predictable response. It was taking all of my strength just to hold Nowzad in place.

It was probably the way I was jigging around trying to restrain my dog that finally caught the guy's attention. He must have wondered what the hell was going on. The handful of chopped sausages that I had been trying to feed Nowzad to distract him now lay discarded in the sand around us.

'It's okay, he won't hurt you,' the young bloke eventually shouted back, seeing his German Shepherd bounding towards me and Nowzad. 'He only wants to play.'

What was wrong with this bloke? Could he not see the straining, snarling bag of attitude and broken teeth that I was fighting a losing battle with to keep under control?

'It isn't *my* dog I'm worried about,' I yelled back, as I stuck a foot out to deflect his dog as it tried to dive on Nowzad.

'You really don't know what you are doing, do you?' I said to the German Shepherd as Nowzad strained every muscle in his body in trying to reach the intruder's head with his teeth. The German Shepherd wasn't listening either and kept diving at us, thinking it was all just a game.

Luckily, each time he did I managed to drag Nowzad to the opposite side of me, keeping him out of reach. But to my utter disbelief, the German Shepherd remained completely oblivious of the danger it was getting itself into: it should have been as obvious as a slap in the face that Nowzad wasn't going to greet it with a friendly sniff of the bum.

I was getting tired of this.

As the German Shepherd's charges continued, I struggled to stay upright as Nowzad twisted and turned, more or less just standing on his rear legs as he lunged again and again.

'NOWZAD!' I cursed as I used my free hand to grab him round his thrashing head as his lower body wrapped round my leg.

By now we were sticking out as clearly as a lighthouse in the middle of the sandy beach, and people were stopping to stare at Nowzad's angry barking and my yelling. It was probably a pretty funny picture, particularly when the force Nowzad was applying as he tried to break away from me was so great that he tripped me over and I landed flat on my back. The image of me lying there with a former Afghan fighting dog wrapped in my arms, thrashing away as it tried desperately to tear itself free, must have been a sight to behold.

Eventually I lost my patience with the young guy who was so blatantly failing to look after his animal.

'Get your dog under control, NOW,' I shouted at him, as I lay on the damp sand struggling to control my own dog.

There was a certain irony to it, even I had to concede.

Yet even then the guy had no idea of the vet treatment his dog was mere seconds away from needing. He leisurely wandered over to his dog as I wrestled like a demon with Nowzad.

'Nowzad, you freaking nightmare, bloody calm down,' I said, trying to sound chilled in the hope it might ease everyone's stress levels. Nor was Nowzad exactly light. With his 36 kilos pressing down on top of me, he really was hard to control. Clamped round him like a limpet, I tried not to swallow the gritty sand lumps that he was flicking into the air with his paws.

To my relief, the German Shepherd was eventually dragged away by the black rope lead that until that point had been dangling uselessly, as some sort of fashion statement, around the lad's neck. As the dog was led a safe distance away, I released Nowzad back to his lead and sat up in the sand.

The Dogs Trust's motto 'A dog is for life, not just for Christmas' has often struck a chord with me. I suppose I couldn't think too ill of the dude with the iPod: at least he was walking the dog (although it would have been nice if he had had more control over it). Far too often I read stories of people who thought a puppy was a good idea at the time and then discarded it without a second thought – most of the UK shelters that were overflowing with unwanted dogs could testify to that.

A dog if treated correctly would be a companion for life. Too many people, from what I could see, would never understand that.

And sadly the strays of Afghanistan would never get the chance to be a 'man's best friend'.

'Having fun, darling?' Lisa asked as she walked Tali back towards me from their vantage point further along the beach.

Fizz Dog and Beamer Boy were running in tight circles around Lisa as they chased each other.

With the excitement of the German Shepherd already forgotten, Nowzad was now madly wagging his stumpy tail at the rest of his pack.

'Nothing I couldn't handle,' I replied nonchalantly as I continued brushing wet sand from my backside and arms.

Thirty seconds ago Nowzad had been a frenzied nightmare. Now he just sat motionless, watching the goings-on of the beach seemingly without a care in the world.

'Yeah, it looked like you were handling it really well from over there,' Lisa said, hiding a grin as she patted Nowzad on the head. I looked at my loving wife with my best non-emotional face.

'Come on, Nowzad, let's get away from these nasty people,' I said as I broke into a gentle jog.

Beamer Boy immediately took up his position in front of us as we pushed off down the beach. After all the excitement of the German Shepherd, Nowzad was obviously relishing the chance to stretch his legs. As usual he ran alongside me doing a waddle-cum-sprint. We didn't stop running until we were both knackered at the end of the beach.

Within only months of the charity starting out it was becoming a lifeline for many soldiers. There were so many of them who had become attached to their stray, four-legged Afghan friend, just as I had with Nowzad, and who needed advice.

Virtually all the militaries operating in Afghanistan enforce a strict policy of 'No feral animals', which I could understand: they were concerned about the spread of disease amongst their troops.

But the policy came to mean that if the charity wanted to stay under the radar, so to speak, and support the guys in keeping their dogs – and then get them to the Afghan Animal Shelter when their tour ended – we had to be very resourceful. It was a tough challenge, particularly given that we were trying to move people and dogs round one of the most hostile areas on the planet.

With the non-secure nature of emails, we were limited to what information the soldiers could give us about their location. On more than one occasion I had combined all my resources and old favours, only to discover that a location was in the middle of absolute nowhere.

This wasn't all bad news, however: the remoteness of a dog's location (and the soldier's post) often meant the soldier would be able to look after his four-legged companion without fear of an over-zealous commander interfering or trying to enforce policy. But the downside was that extracting the dog and getting it to the safety of the north of the country and the Afghan rescue centre – the exact location of which we had to keep secret so as to protect it from possible Taliban reprisals – was incredibly difficult.

For the locals, carrying a dog could have severe consequences if the dog was discovered during a routine search at any of the numerous Taliban checkpoints that were still in operation: the Taliban view on dogs was not the best and meant severe punishment awaited anybody who ignored their command. The Taliban still managed to guard several of the many barren valleys that lead to the north. And most unaffiliated Afghans didn't need money that badly to risk transporting dogs across Taliban territory.

I find it hard to write emails that often have to explain the hopelessness of the situation. Tapping out the words 'Sorry, but there really is nothing more we can do' is soul destroying, especially as I know exactly what that dog means to the soldier and how much it will hurt to leave their four-legged buddy behind. Over the time the charity's been running for, we have received several emails from soldiers who were just too deep in the bad guys' back garden for us to help them. When this happens, there is just nothing we can do.

As Valentine's day approached Fubar had become my main focus as far as the charity went. We'd finally got her on the move, but it had been a long struggle.

Our first problem had been that we didn't know precisely where Chris was in Afghanistan. So we had wasted precious days sending emails back and forth trying to actually establish Fubar's location.

As was so often the case with the six or seven rescues that we had been asked to perform over the last seven or so months, the situation had been left to the eleventh hour. Coupled with this, the emails, as ever, lacked the information necessary for us to make an immediate assessment of whether we could actually get to the dog or not. (Over the months we have run the charity for, we have often toyed with the idea of renaming ourselves 'lastminutedogrescue.com'.)

Jacs and Wrinkle, two dogs destined for America we had assisted in the rescues of, had been no different. Thankfully, both of these dogs were now residents of the Afghan rescue shelter while we arranged their onward journeys in relative slow time compared to the urgency of the initial move. Jacs was half white over the front of his body whereas the rest of him – his back legs and tail – were covered in a light tan-coloured hair. His face was divided perfectly by a white line that separated the patches around his eyes. Wrinkle had been discovered by a civilian contractor. Immediately on looking at the pup you would be drawn in by his deep blue eyes that seemed to be smiling at you as with minimal effort the little pup wormed his way into your heart.

Without Chris being too specific in detail, we discovered where Fubar actually was, only to realise that any transport requests for her were going to be difficult, to say the least. It was a tough one.

I sensed that Chris had just been glad that we were here to email with. We had given him the hope that until now had been missing. And I knew precisely how he felt. I had spent many cold nights alone in the makeshift dog run next to Nowzad, gazing up at the crystal-clear night sky and the thousands of twinkling stars, hoping they'd magically reveal how I was to get the dog that had become my mate to the safety of the Afghan rescue centre.

Chris and the Dutch lads had had an equally frustrating time. With their military command point-blank refusing to assist – even after a newspaper campaign back in the Netherlands had been launched to support Fubar – Chris emailed that he had been close to admitting defeat. But we had given him fresh hope, and his words had fired me up, too. I was just hoping we could make a difference. This was, after all, why I had set up Nowzad Dogs in the first place.

But I was also fearful. I didn't want to be responsible for getting Fubar killed, whether it was because she escaped from the transport we arranged to take her from the Dutch base to the rescue or through disease once she was meant to be safely there.

And my fears only deepened as we tried to get the Afghan rescue centre involved. Even though ISAF had been mounting their campaign in Afghanistan since 2002, the situation in northern Afghanistan, where the rescue centre was based, had worsened. The Taliban were resurgent again and there had been several high-profile bombings.

Koshan, the local Afghan who had become our invaluable ally in managing the place and communicating with us, told us that he could not make the full journey southward to collect Fubar. It had become more and more obvious that it would have to be another local who did the job and transported Fubar north. This was not good news.

As I knew from my experience with Nowzad, fate sometimes conjures up the most unlikely solutions. In my case, it had been the arrival of a taxi – finally arranged by the local Afghan Police commander on my final day in the Now Zad compound – the driver of which had agreed to transport all my dogs to link up with another driver also organised by the Police commander to finish their journey to the rescue centre.

I suggested to Chris that he might want to try the same thing with the Afghans he worked with. From Chris's emails I sensed he had treated the Afghan Army ranks well during his tour with them, and I knew from my time there that most trusted and respected any man who put his life on the line while they attempted to rid their country of the Taliban. The guys he knew would feel they owed Chris.

Thankfully for all concerned, the Afghan Army guys came up with a solution. They promised to transport Fubar to Kandahar, and a civilian construction worker would then transport Fubar to a collection point with Koshan.

The timing was like something from a Hollywood movie. It all happened as the clock ticked down to Chris's departure back to the Netherlands. In fact, Chris had to leave the patrol base the day before Fubar was due to be picked up. He wrote that he played with and made a fuss of Fubar for the last time, before walking out of the operation room, his assault rifle slung over his shoulder. He had no option but to trust the arrangements the ANA had put in place.

He went through the slow agony of catching up on Fubar's progress during his long journey home to the Netherlands. He knew that whether he would see Fubar again was out of his hands. There was nothing more he could do.

I understood all too well the mix of hope and despair that he must have been feeling. I had been through it myself after I had sent off my group of dogs, including

Nowzad and Tali. The fact that I had physically seen them off as they left in the taxi had, I suppose, given me some consolation, but not much. Especially when I found out that not all of the Now Zad pack had made it to the safety of the rescue centre. Immediately images of RPG and AK appeared as I begun to question what I had done. Maybe I had done the wrong thing. Perhaps I should have let them be, left them to survive in the landscape in which they'd been born. Maybe I shouldn't have interfered. These and other doubts had assailed me as I had made my long journey back to the UK as my tour had finished.

On more than one occasion I have found myself thinking these thoughts when sitting with Nowzad since. The guilt comes piling in on me and I find myself apologising to him. 'Sorry I couldn't save your buddy, Nowzie,' I whisper as I stroke his stumpy ears. Of course, I know he doesn't understand what I am talking about, but sometimes I wish he did, as perhaps he would tell me I did the right thing, and limit the guilt I feel.

As we waited for news of Fubar, we were in constant touch with Koshan. I was continually checking my email and mobile phone for any updates.

Finally after what felt like weeks but was only days, we received the news that Fubar had made it safely to the Afghan rescue centre. I felt a familiar mixture of joy, relief and responsibility. We had got her this far. Now we just had to keep her safe and healthy and finish the job: we had to get her on a plane and out of Afghanistan.

The message had also reached Chris, who by now was taking a two-day rest stop in Crete on his way back to the Netherlands. But the joy the news about Fubar brought him had been tempered by other, less happy news that had reached him from Afghanistan. His good friend, another serving Dutch marine, had been killed by an IED the same day that Fubar had made it to the Afghan rescue centre.

As always when we received news of a dog making it to the Afghan rescue centre, the charity had to step up a gear. We weren't always involved in all the rescues from the start. Sometimes we were drafted in to lend support at the request of Koshan, normally when an American soldier was struggling to fund the final leg of the rescue operation.

This was where our charity really came into its own. We'd promote the needy Afghan dog's story on our website, and I'd talk about them at one of the local slideshows I'd started giving, and then many hours were spent writing out thank you notes to acknowledge the donations that arrived.

So now as the message from Koshan arrived in the inbox confirming that Fubar had made it to the safety of the shelter it was time for us to come into our own and arrange the next phase of the operation. But this time we had double the work to do.

With his last email, Koshan had also included details of a dog called Beardog. I looked at the pictures of the oversized animal that was staring back at me from the email.

It wasn't a dog. It was, surely, a large, dark brown horse trying its best to disguise itself as a dog.

With closely cropped ears and docked tail, and a streak of white running along the underside of its body, the animal was a massive version of Nowzad. Yet Koshan had described him as a puppy.

Keeping it brief, he explained that Beardog had been brought to the shelter by an English soldier who had found him wandering alone along an Afghan alley, apparently just after being cruelly relieved of his ears.

I wasn't sure how the soldier had known about the Afghan animal shelter, we did our best not to advertise the location as it could become a potential soft target for the Taliban, but without knowing what else to do, the soldier had dropped the pup at Koshan's door. And that, as it turned out, had been nearly four months ago.

I don't know why Koshan hadn't told us about the Beardog situation any earlier but it was too late to worry about that now. The cute little pup without any ears wasn't a cute little pup any more. It was a Beardog. Its great big head seemed to launch itself out of the digital photo on the computer screen in 3D.

With room at the shelter at a premium, Koshan needed our help. As the soldier who had left him there had not been back in touch, without our intervention Beardog would have to be released back on to the Afghan streets. There was nothing else Koshan could do.

It took me only seconds to decide that the charity would

take Beardog on. I just hoped that as he was still only really a young pup, he wouldn't be bringing any of the baggage with him that had accompanied Nowzad.

We soon got into our stride with what would rapidly become a familiar routine. We first had to compare flight prices, arrange transportation to and from airports and seek out quarantine facilities near the dog's eventual destination. All time-consuming, and expensive, stuff. Depending on exchanges rates, we wouldn't get much change from £3,000.

Sometimes it was hard to justify that expense to people who didn't understand the bond that could grow between a soldier and a stray dog. I was all too aware how many good things we could do with that amount of money at shelters in the UK. But with publicity, people donated money because they were concerned for the plight of that one particular Afghan dog. And who was I to put a price on the life of an Afghan stray?

I received one letter from a gentleman called Pete. Reading his hand-written note, I discovered he had served in 1947 in what had then been called the North West Frontier, a place that we now know of as the Pakistan–Afghanistan tribal border areas.

A faded black-and-white photograph of a dog sitting upright on the veranda of an old India-Colonial style army barracks had fallen from the envelope. The animal looked proud, the white-coloured patch on its chest standing out strongly as it studied something off in the distance. The dog was the spit of Jena, one of the dogs that we had rescued from Now Zad and re-homed successfully in America, except the dog in the photograph had lived nearly 60 years ago.

The dog had been called Scruffy and from what I could gather, had been instrumental in the morale of Pete and his mates as they served in a foreign land, far from home; the high-tech communications that made service life bearable today were all but non-existent back then.

Pete had simply stated what so many of the other letters did: '*Here is my small donation to making sure you help as many Afghan strays get home.*' Scruffy had not come home with Pete. I guessed he was making amends.

Donations like Pete's were crucial if we were going to be able to pay for the various forms of transport that would be needed to get Fubar and Beardog back to the west.

With this in mind, the website would need updating with a brief written piece about Fubar and how Chris had come to care for her, and the short tale of Beardog. Most importantly, we needed to get up some photos of the cute, underfed little white dog. A picture was worth a thousand words (especially when those words were mine). We needed to tug at people's heartstrings and get them to raise the large amount of money that I knew we needed.

We quickly discovered that Dutch quarantine law was a breeze compared to the UK. But time wasn't on our side, and the paperwork proved too much, especially as it was all in Dutch. We quickly worked out that it would be easier to arrange for young Fubar to enter the UK quarantine

system for three months while we arranged the transportation required getting her to the Netherlands, and with
Beardog sharing her quarantine run, we would receive a
much-needed discount. She would then be required to
spend just 11 days in quarantine upon arrival in the
Netherlands. Not only that, she could spend those 11 days
at home, which I couldn't believe.

'Just 11 days of quarantine, Nowzad, how easy would
that have been, eh?' I asked the sleeping Afghan dog who
was currently keeping my feet warm as I read through yet
another website full of red tape and rules. 'We'd have saved
a bloody fortune in fuel.'

The biggest headache now was the detailed DEFRA paperwork.

My first dealing with a DEFRA vet had not been good.
His lack of knowledge about rabies and the required paperwork for a dog to enter the UK had been slightly unnerving.
Luckily I had persevered and the second DEFRA vet had
been extremely helpful. Since then I had become something
of an expert at picking my way through the minefield of
admin that was required. And besides, I had the fantastic
support of Rebecca at the quarantine centre. She had
completed the required paperwork a thousand times over and
laughed at the complexities of importing a dog into the UK.

I had soon organised a joint plan and sent emails to
Chris, and then the necessary emails booking transport and
flights and the all-important quarantine booking.

As the computer made the familiar pinging sound to let me know the email had been sent safely, I flopped back into the chair and gave Nowzad's head a ruffle.

'It sure doesn't get any easier moving your mates around,' I said with a sigh.

CHAPTER SEVEN

Advanced Classes

'Lisa, come and have a look at this,' I shouted without moving from my chair in front of the computer screen. 'Somebody's having a laugh.' It was only just over two months after Nowzad and Tali had arrived home with us. And I couldn't believe my eyes.

'It's okay. I've got a barrel full of them down here,' she shouted back. 'I'm clearing up after your dogs. Again.'

Sure enough, when I stuck my head round the corner of the spare-room door and looked downstairs, I could see Lisa on her hands and knees scrubbing away at a wet patch she'd just discovered on the hallway carpet.

I made a strategic withdrawal and headed back to the computer to reread the email. I didn't want to be accused of interfering, did I?

Rather than shouting down again, I printed out the email in the hope that by the time I had run it off, Lisa would have finished her cleaning duties and be more receptive. It was worth a try.

'All right, I am coming to you,' I said in my most

charming voice, before bounding down the stairs with the single sheet of A4 paper.

'What's so important it can't wait?' Lisa asked without looking up from her scrubbing.

I thrust the printout into her wet hand. Lisa stopped cleaning long enough to read the email.

'Somebody *is* having a laugh,' she said.

'I'm sure that's what I said,' I replied, moving nimbly round the wet patch to get to the kitchen and make us both a cup of tea.

Lisa dropped the cloth back into the bowl of disinfectant and leant back against the doorway to the under-stairs cupboard. We both looked at each other, and then at Nowzad, then back at each other.

'Nowzad, you're apparently going to be the star of the biggest dog show on the planet,' Lisa said to the large, inanimate creature lying on the carpet a few yards away. 'We're going to Crufts!'

Every year, the Kennel Club hosts 'Crufts', a four-day extravaganza at Birmingham's National Exhibition Centre (the NEC) to crown the best in breed of the hundreds of dogs that enter. For most dog owners it is dog Heaven, while others seem to despise it with a passion due to the minority of breeders that were apparently still using outdated and harmful breeding practices in their quest to own the best dog of its breed. If it was true it still wasn't my fight. We had enough on our plate with Afghanistan.

Apart from anything else, Lisa and I had never been, let alone as guests of the show's organisers. According to the email, Nowzad had been selected as one of the five finalists in something called the *Friends for Life* award for 2008. Apparently the prize celebrated the dog heroes in everyday life. Not that Afghanistan was typical of everyday life for most, but I could see where they were going with it.

Apart from giving Lisa and me a nice day out, I quickly saw that it handed us a fantastic opportunity to promote the charity: I imagined one of the organisers must have read about Nowzad's amazing story in one of the recent news-paper articles that covered the launch of the charity. The winning dog for the *Friends for Life* award was to be decided on finals night at Crufts, via a public phone vote. Surely they would give us a chance to talk a bit about Nowzad and how he got to England? We could mention the charity then and get some much-needed free publicity for it. We were both slightly concerned at how we would fit everything in. It would probably affect the workload involved with arranging everything for Fubar and Beardog, but we thought it was worth it. We could do both, couldn't we?

As my mind raced away in one direction, Lisa's was heading in another, perhaps more practical direction. As she reread the email she began shaking her head. 'Are you seriously considering taking Nowzad into the middle of Crufts, amongst thousands of people and dogs?' she asked me eventually. 'We can't even walk down the beach without him turning into a freak show.'

Lisa had a point, but by now I wasn't listening. 'Think of the publicity the charity will gain, honey,' I said softly as I stroked the top of Nowzad's head. 'We couldn't pay for that: it will be Nowzad's way of helping out the buddies we left behind,' I added.

Lisa took her mug of tea and sipped at it contemplatively. As she did so, however, her head was still rocking disapprovingly from one side to the other. 'Yeah, I can't wait for Nowzad to eat somebody on live TV,' she said, straight-faced.

The next few days went by in a flurry of email activity as we found out more about the potential bear pit that we would be dropping Nowzad into.

The more we learned, the more jittery we both became.

The *Friends for Life* final was going to be filmed live on the night and broadcast on the BBC. So we didn't even have the comfort of knowing that any of Nowzad's misdemeanours could be safely edited out of the show.

If he did something bad, we'd get more publicity than we could ever have bargained for. And not in a good way, I imagined.

A day or two after the initial invitation, the organisers somehow realised that Nowzad was actually only one of the Afghan refugees we had under our roof. 'Great news, Lisa,' I announced gleefully as she stumbled through the door after a particularly frustrating day attempting to get young naval recruits into some sort of shape. 'Crufts want us to take Tali as well.'

'Hoofing,' she said, throwing me a look as she dropped her day sack on the kitchen floor. 'You really don't like making things easy, do you?'

Yet again Lisa had a point. I had volunteered us to take two nightmares into the bear pit.

'Bugger,' I said as I slowly realised just how difficult it was very likely going to be.

Not that anything looked that difficult at the moment. A few feet away from me, Nowzad was sitting perfectly still while Tali charged and battered him as she tempted him to play. Nowzad was having none of it. He steadfastly ignored her advances while he waited patiently for me or Lisa to move. He knew what he wanted. And we knew what he was waiting for.

He had been expecting us to say, 'We're home, dogs!' and offer him a small, gravy-flavoured dog biscuit as we did every evening when we returned from work. Instead, we completely forgot to do so as we discussed our options.

'Nowzad, I think we need to take you to training classes,' Lisa said.

'Better give that Helen a call,' I nodded.

Just a few days earlier, we had received an email from a dog-loving woman called Helen. She had contacted us on behalf of Just Dogs, a dog-training club that had decided to offer Nowzad and Tali free sessions after reading about them in the local paper.

I pinged off an email to her that night, taking her up on

her kind offer. The reply had come bouncing back almost immediately. She sounded over the moon, if a little shocked at the revelation that we were contemplating taking the dogs to Crufts.

As we pressed on with the arrangements, Helen sent me the times and dates for when she said she wanted Nowzad and Tali to come along to her classes.

'The advanced classes start at seven o'clock in the evening,' she said.

'The advanced class?' I asked, suddenly confused. 'Are you sure, Helen? They're not the best behaved of dogs.' I was lucky if these two Afghan nightmares sat on command first time: they were most definitely not advanced-class material. Nor did I want to be responsible for Helen's loss of accreditation as a dog trainer.

'No, the advanced class will be better for them because the other dogs are easy to control,' Helen said.

'Oh, right, I see,' I said, trying to hide the embarrassment in my voice. I should have thought of that.

Helen explained directions to the venue for the classes; a barn on a farm near Feniton, just outside Honiton, about half an hour from our house.

'See you there,' I said. 'But don't blame me for the carnage!'

It was dark as we drove along the gravel driveway that led to the farm where Helen had asked us to turn up for the training classes.

Even though the car park area was poorly lit, we could still make out plenty of other vehicles, which translated into plenty of dogs for Nowzad to get stuck into.

'Maybe this is a bad idea,' I said to Lisa as I pulled the van into an available space.

'Too late for that now,' Lisa replied as she opened the side door of our van to let the dogs out. 'Come on, nightmares; let's see how you get on.'

Helen was waiting for us at the door to the barn as we walked across the car park towards the large building, from which light was spilling out into the darkness.

For some reason, it reminded me of the locations used by mad scientists in kids' cartoons, carrying out secret experiments. Come to think of it, I finally agreed with Lisa. We probably were mad for agreeing to take Nowzad and Tali to Crufts, and even more insane to bring them along to a dog-training class.

There were so many doubts in my mind. Could Nowzad and Tali be socialised with other dogs? Was Nowzad going to completely freak out the other dogs and their owners?

It was going to be crazy finding out.

Expert trainer that she was, Helen held her distance as we came towards her so that Nowzad wouldn't lunge at her. I had briefed her on what to expect but she hadn't sounded too concerned on the phone, and she seemed equally calm now.

'Nowzad, this is Helen, she is going to turn you into a loving and sociable dog,' I said sarcastically as Nowzad stood his ground, sniffing the air with suspicion. 'Yeah, right,' he might have been saying.

The sounds of firm commands being issued were clearly audible from within the barn, so I guessed the dogs inside were already being put through their paces.

Helen knelt down and offered Nowzad a treat from her outstretched hand. 'How are you doing, Nowzad?'

Nowzad eyed the treat carefully. For a stray that had been brought up fighting for survival, always hunting for scraps, Nowzad was a gentle giant when it came to taking treats from somebody's hand. He never, ever snatched. It was one of his little quirks, one that always made me smile. To me it was just further evidence that, deep inside, there was a great dog struggling to find its way out.

Nowzad sniffed at Helen's hand once more before carefully nibbling the treat.

'I thought you said he was a monster dog?' Helen said as she stood up.

'Just wait,' I smiled in the gloom. 'Nowzad won't let us down.'

Now it wasn't pride but pure dread that I was feeling.

Helen had explained that we would go in once the class was under way. The idea was that we were not actually going to take part in any of the lesson; we were just going to use the opportunity to stroll round the outside of the training group so that Nowzad and Tali could get used to the environment, much the same as they would when we got to Crufts.

Helen handed over a pocketful of the pungent-smelling mucky treats that she had just fed Nowzad.

'Homemade baked garlic tripe biscuits,' she said as I fed Nowzad one, while Lisa did the same with Tali.

'Smells nice,' I replied politely.

As Helen opened the large barn door, Morag, a fellow trainer, warned the members of the dog class that we were coming in. They had, apparently, been well briefed on our arrival and what to expect.

Inside the barn, there was a real mix of dogs. A range of breeds, from a Scots Terrier to a German Shepherd, made up the eight or so dogs of the class.

Out of habit, I quickly checked the exit and entry points. There was only one: the door that we had just walked through and which was now firmly shut behind us.

Stacked up against the right-hand side of the barn were several dog ramps, mini jumps and hooped folding tunnels for use in the agility class. But I was under no illusions. Nowzad would not require their use any time soon.

I realised that Morag's warning was less to warn the owners about us and more to ensure that all class members had their pets on a lead. I was reassured to know that none of the other dogs in the class would be loose. There would be no repeat of the episode at the beach.

The assembled club members all nodded hello but a few of them seemed unimpressed by Nowzad's reputation. As if to prove it was well deserved, he started christening the barn door. The floor of the barn was covered in small woodchips, which Nowzad immediately sent flying in the air as he flicked his back legs several times having finished.

'Wow,' Helen said as she was covered in woodchips as she passed behind him. Nowzad did have a powerful flick; I had to give him that. Both Tali and I had been on the receiving end of it several times.

'Yeah, sorry about that,' I apologised.

Nowzad was already eyeballing the other dogs as they wandered round the barn with their owners. They were all tight on their leads, under the direction of Helen who was standing in the middle of the barn.

Everything seemed fine, but now and again Nowzad would catch sight of the large brown-black German Shepherd, and would suddenly lunge in its direction before I could bring him back under control.

The young German Shepherd didn't even flinch. It just carried on trotting round the ring as if the angry Afghan dog was just a minor annoyance that was to be ignored. Tali on the other hand seemed quite content with Lisa, and was just trotting round the outside area of the dog class, sniffing the wood chips as she went.

'Nowzad, chill out,' I yelled as he lunged for the German Shepherd as it came round again.

'Pen, feed him one of those treats and turn his head away,' Helen said as Nowzad strained to get away from me. He really didn't like the dog.

'Here, eat this, evil dog,' I said as I stuffed a tripe treat into Nowzad's mouth. I knew I shouldn't have worn my best jeans for this; my pocket would be stained for life.

I dragged Nowzad round so he was facing the barn wall. He kept struggling to turn his head back towards the group and in particular the German Shepherd, even though everybody there was blatantly ignoring us.

'More treats,' Helen smiled.

I fed Nowzad two more, which settled him enough for me to move him in the opposite direction from the dogs.

'Take him round the outside of the group, keep talking to him and distract him every now and again with treats as you go,' was Helen's advice.

'Okay,' I replied as I led Nowzad off clockwise round the group.

While I was struggling with Nowzad, Lisa was still having a great time with Tali.

She was happily following along by Lisa's side and really didn't seem to have much interest in any of the other hounds.

As for them, I couldn't actually see why they were at the class; they all seemed extremely well trained to me already.

'That is what you should be like, mate,' I said to Nowzad as I stifled one of his potential pounces at the German Shepherd yet again.

I didn't hold out much hope that Nowzad would turn out anything like as well trained as the Alsatian. I tried to offer a sincere, apologetic smile to the female owner as we passed each other.

'Treats,' Helen yelled across the room.

I watched as nearly every owner immediately fished in their pockets for a smelly dog treat for their canine pal. Nowzad just looked longingly at my pocket.

'No, I meant just Pen,' Helen shouted again.

'Sorry,' I said stupidly as I reached for a treat for the drooling dog by my side.

I slipped Nowzad a treat as Lisa mouthed 'Loser' across the barn at me.

'Love you too, honey,' I mouthed back as the stern eye of Helen bore down on me.

'Just who is taking who for a walk here, Pen?' Helen asked, stopping short of me again so as not to tempt Nowzad.

I think she already knew the answer.

Before I could make up some jolly excuse, Helen was already taking charge. 'Nowzad, sit,' she commanded as she held out a treat.

To my amazement, Nowzad sat immediately and waited quietly for the approaching tripe biscuit.

'Good boy,' Helen said as she patted him on the head. 'Right, Pen, make him sit every time he gets a treat and keep him occupied. Don't let him fix on that dog,' she explained, a big smile on her face.

I felt I was the one being trained rather than Nowzad. In a way I suppose I was. Over the months that Nowzad had been living with us I had probably been soft with him.

'No,' I thought to myself, there was no doubt: I was soft

with him. I knew I shouldn't have been, but it felt like Nowzad deserved some decent down time after all he had been through back in Afghanistan. But I now realised that allowing him to get away with everything was not going to help him adapt to his new life with us.

Helen had managed to control Nowzad, even if it was just getting him to sit on command, within only minutes of meeting the Afghan stray.

'Okay, Nowzad, time we got serious, eh?' I said to him as I patted him on the head while he was still sitting to attention.

The session continued for another half an hour, with Nowzad and Tali mingling quite nicely, under control, with the training class. Helen and Morag even halted the class and arranged the other dogs in two lines so that the two Afghan hounds could walk down between them. And with treats on demand to distract Nowzad while I did my best to be strict with him, we even managed to walk within two feet of the German Shepherd without a confrontation.

Maybe Nowzad wasn't the nightmare I had imagined after all, I thought. Maybe it was all me. Deep down I knew I would just have to treat Nowzad as if he was one of my troop of marines. Nowzad needed discipline and once he paid attention to me then I could make a fuss of him.

Attending the Just Dogs training classes each week added to what we considered to be an already packed weekly schedule. It was pretty hectic to get home from work, take the dogs out for a decent walk, grab something to eat and then load Nowzad and Tali into the van for the drive to the class, but it was worth it.

There were good signs of progress. Nowzad's stumpy tail would wag madly at the sight of Helen, mainly because he knew she was clutching garlic baked treats in her outstretched hand. But for every one step forward there was often another backward one, and Nowzad still lunged at most of the dogs and their owners attending the class.

'Maybe they just want to lick all the other dogs?' I said to Lisa one week as she just managed to swirl Tali out of the way of a big St Bernard that was blocking their path as they walked round the class. Tali was a pain when she was with Nowzad but fine on her own. I figured she saw him as a big brother and together they would take on the dog world.

I had a very strong feeling that most of the owners didn't believe that Nowzad and Tali, the two most disruptive pupils of the class, were going to behave in the main arena of Crufts on finals night.

'I think they think we're mad,' I said to Helen as we walked in and around the patiently waiting class, belt-feeding Nowzad garlic treats from my pocket like a machine gun.

'You are mad,' Helen replied simply.

Away from the twice-weekly training classes, any spare minute at home or work was taken up with the ever-changing arrangements for Fubar and Beardog's transportation to the

UK. I was also somehow answering the ever-increasing build-up of charity mail arriving on our doorstep.

Any prospect of Lisa and me having time for ourselves was completely out of the question. Our days were just an endless blur of non-stop activity. From the moment the shrill beep of the bedside alarm pierced the early-morning darkness, until the moment we flicked off the bedroom light as we finally collapsed at the end of the day 18 hours later, every single second was occupied. Both of us were close to being swamped with a combination of real work, dog walking and charity time.

Secretly, I think we were both hoping that once we had been to the madness of the biggest dog show on earth, the publicity and interest surrounding the charity would ease slightly, allowing us to take a breather for a while.

But as the workload continued to build, reality was slowly dawning. It hit me one night after I had been on the computer for what seemed like ten hours straight. I hadn't even managed to get out of my uniform after arriving home from work.

'Who am I trying to kid?' I asked Lisa. 'It isn't going to ease off after Crufts, is it?'

She just looked at me and smiled as she emptied a new sack of mail, letters and parcels spilling into the middle of the living-room carpet.

'Just so you know; it was your idea,' Lisa noted, smiling serenely.

I couldn't say very much in reply to that.

CHAPTER EIGHT

Out of Control

Thanks to another mini-mutiny in the kitchen during feeding time, I knew I was already running late for work. Again.

As a physical-training instructor in the Marines, failing to arrive on time was never a good move. The usual punishment was two lengths of front crawl in the 'tank', an outdoor pool that was used to catch marine recruits if they fell from the high rope obstacle used during their assault-course training. As an added evil bonus for instructors, we would be expected to swim wearing our uniform.

Yet despite all this, I couldn't resist it. As I got ready for a quick shower I turned the time sucker on.

The time sucker was what Lisa and I had come to call the computer as it had the habit of sucking up time in a way that was beyond belief.

I jumped in the shower while the computer warmed up and it was ready and waiting to time-sucker me as I pulled on my uniform, my spare set placed on the bed to take with me in the eventuality I was required to undertake an individual medley in the outside tank.

'I can still do it; I'll quickly give the emails a once-over,' I thought, looking at my watch as I plonked myself down in the swivel chair.

But the first email that appeared dragged me in immediately. It was the message's title that caught and held me: Blue the Afghan dog it simply said.

As I began reading I saw that it was from an American soldier who was caring for an Afghan dog named Blue. As I read on, however, I began to ask myself whether it was Blue the dog who was caring for the American soldier.

From the accompanying photograph, Blue looked typical of an Afghan stray: his light brown coat had darker patches of brown that also covered his ears and the end of his snout. He also had sad eyes.

From the tone of the emails, I guessed that that soldier's unit was having a tough time of it. Especially as American tours of duty in Afghanistan last for a year, unlike their European counterparts who only have to complete six months.

Blue sounded a splendid dog, always bouncing around and happy to see the soldiers when they returned from patrols; he had become the cheerful face amongst the dangerous sea of mistrust they felt when they left the security of their well-defended base.

The soldier's mother was keenly following Blue's story, too. I felt that with the obvious concern she felt for her son serving in Afghanistan she was grateful for the comfort he had found in the form of the Afghan dog.

I quickly contacted Koshan at the rescue shelter to discuss if it was possible for a driver to reach Blue and the soldier's current location. Having done what I needed to do to get the ball rolling, I pressed the send button and looked at my watch again.

'I am definitely going to be late,' I said to myself.

I could already feel the icy cold of the tank. It was going to be a long swim.

It might have been Saturday morning but there was no peace for the wicked. With the emails and paperwork that the charity was generating, Lisa had volunteered to take all four dogs down to the beach so that I could try and get on top of the Matterhorn of admin that was piling up. The idea was that we would then have the opportunity to spend the afternoon doing something on our own that didn't involve computers or dogs, but probably did involve chilling out and having a few beers.

Dog walks in our household usually follow the same pattern. Carnage breaks out in the kitchen when the four musketeers realise there's a walk on the cards, with Fizz Dog leading the barking chorus, as ever.

If getting the dogs out of the house for a walk is hard work, getting them into the van is even more chaotic. Fizz Dog and Beamer Boy usually charge for the van, where it's parked at the end of the garden path. The sliding van door is always opened before they're let into the garden, so they can dive straight on to the towel-covered rear seat. All you can see is a mass of flailing legs as both dogs scrap for the window seat. Fizz Dog always prevails, however. And at this particular moment, a squirrel could come up and shout boo at her and Fizz Dog would just ignore it, such is her focus on claiming the window seat.

On this particular day, with Tali dancing round and round in circles and getting underfoot, it was easier for me just to pick her up and carry her out to the van than attempt to walk her there. Meanwhile, Lisa clipped Nowzad into his smart blue body harness. She was not going to take any chances where he was concerned.

With the whole pack safely installed in the van, I slammed the sliding door shut and kissed Lisa goodbye.

'Fifty emails and letters, darling,' she said, referring to the current pile stacked on the dining-room table.

'No problem, honey bear,' I lied. Even with the peace and quiet of no dogs in the house, I would never get 50 emails done. That was definitely pushing it.

As I walked back through the kitchen door and turned to close it, I noticed Tali's body harness on the work surface by the sink. I had forgotten to fit it round Tali before I had picked her up.

'Oh, bugger,' I said out loud.

Lisa would get to the beach and Tali would only have her thin collar to clip the lead to. Lisa knew how clever Tali was at slipping her collar, and I assumed she would be forced to leave 'the Taliban' in the van. She wouldn't risk walking her.

For a moment I wondered about ringing her to let her know, but she would already have hit the traffic that accumulated on Saturdays; it took long enough as it was to drive to the beach, and I doubted very much whether Lisa would consider driving back home to collect the harness.

As I headed upstairs to the office, I was certain of one thing. I was not going to be flavour of the month. Again.

As the computer screen displayed email after email, I tried to concentrate on my replies while keeping one eye on my mobile phone just in case Lisa decided to call.

It remained silent.

My biggest concern at the moment was still Blue, the American soldier's dog. Since we'd first communicated with the soldier, we'd got the wheels turning on getting Blue to the Afghan rescue centre. I had liaised with Koshan, the centre's manager. He was more than happy to accept Blue into the centre but, as ever, getting the dog to him would be the big problem.

To complicate matters further, as the emails had flown back and forth, another problem had arisen. Blue had started to develop skin lesions round his eyes and nose. From the descriptions the soldier sent us, it hadn't sounded that bad at the start so I was not unduly worried. But it wasn't something that should be left to fester. After all this was Afghanistan.

I knew that the soldier did not have access to a vet or medicines, so I urged him to do everything possible to locate a friendly Afghan driver who would be willing to transport the dog to the rescue shelter. At least there Blue would have a chance of being seen by a vet.

As we corresponded, I could sense the inner conflict going on in the soldier's mind. It was all too familiar to me. I had gone through it myself when I had been in Now Zad, agonising over whether to risk sending my dogs halfway across the country to the centre.

The soldier was thinking exactly what I had thought: did he send Blue on a dangerous journey, one that potentially could result in his death, or did he hold on to him a while longer, caring for him as well as he could?

It was a heart-rending choice to make and I couldn't make it for him. But I had a gut feeling that if he didn't get Blue to the centre soon, the dog would suffer.

I was snapped out of my thoughts by the sounds from outside of the van door sliding open and the loud barking of four dogs.

Lisa was standing by the back door with her none-too-impressed face on. She was holding Tali's harness. Tali was standing next to her, looking extremely subdued.

'This might have saved me from the disaster that I've just had,' Lisa said, shaking the rig at me.

'Oops, did you leave that here?' I asked innocently. 'Why didn't you ring me? I would have brought it down.'

'Because I was too busy chasing dogs all over the beach, that's why,' Lisa replied, throwing me a look that should have turned me to stone.

A few moments later, nursing the cup of tea that I had rustled up for her, she told me what had happened.

At the beach, and noticing that Tali was missing a vital piece of her beachwear, my name had apparently quickly been associated with some unrepeatable obscenities.

Lisa decided that she wasn't about to drive all the way home, so she had thought she would risk it and walk Tali with just her thin collar.

'I planned on keeping Tali walking forward on a tight lead,' Lisa sighed. 'I know what she's like slipping out of that collar. I wasn't going to let her get behind me.' Fizz Dog and Beamer Boy had pegged it off down the beach as Lisa had walked with Nowzad and Tali on their leads. Within two yards of hitting the sand Nowzad was already cocking his leg and claiming a new piece of ground.

Tali calming trotted alongside Lisa, seemingly quite happy to walk calmly along the beach as every 200 yards or so they arrived at the thick wooden barriers that divided the beach to protect the expanse of golden sand from the eroding effects of the strong tides that ran the length of the beach.

Both Fizz Dog and Beamer Boy had easily cleared the two-foot-high barriers as if running in the Grand National. Nowzad had preferred a slight run up, before stopping suddenly, and weeing on the green slime-covered wood.

Finally, with a monstrous effort he had lunged himself up and over the top to land unceremoniously on the other side.

It had been while Lisa waited for Nowzad to have a pee that Tali had seen the young brown seagull perched on top of a nearby groyne.

Tali loved birds. But not in the ornithological sense.

Before Lisa could react, Tali had slipped her collar and was sprinting towards the bird.

Now Tali was quick, real quick.

But still she was no match for a young seagull, especially one with a head start and wings. The bird stretched out and launched itself into the air in a slow graceful take-off as it spied the approaching manic dog.

Fizz Dog and Beamer Boy had still been running in the opposite direction when they heard Lisa screaming their names over the whooshing of the onshore wind.

Both dogs turned on the spot and charged back the way they had come in pursuit of Lisa and a former Afghan fighting dog that hadn't moved that fast for a long time, if ever, as they set off after Tali.

Tali was leaping the sea-drenched wooden barriers with ease as she continued to chase the seagull.

Lisa had a split-second realisation: there was no time to stop and tie Nowzad to a groyne, as the athletic Tali would be long gone by the time she could resume the chase. Lisa needed a miracle. And then one happened.

The seagull turned out to sea. As it did, so did Tali who began skipping across the rocks that jutted out in the oncoming swell. In the midst of her blind craze to catch the seagull she forgot to keep looking where she was headed.

So Tali ran straight off the end of the rocks and ploughed headlong into the sea.

Tali had never been swimming before, as far as we knew, anyway. She had begun to panic, her legs floundering away like mad below the surface as she desperately tried to turn around. She had just worked out that this wasn't an option when the cavalry arrived in the form of Lisa, who had waded into the freezing sea and grabbed the flailing dog. Amazingly, Nowzad had remained safely attached to her free hand.

When Lisa looked up, she discovered a small crowd of fellow dog walkers that had gathered to watch the unfolding drama. Fizz Dog and Beamer Boy were calmly sitting in front of the crowd, as bemused as any of the humans by the crazy goings-on.

I did feel slightly guilty at forgetting to fit Tali's harness. But I couldn't prevent the giggles that were slowly forming, no matter how hard I tried to stop them.

I knew I was going to get a slap. I just didn't know how hard it was going to be.

Fubar and Beardog arrived at the quarantine centre during the early part of March 2008 and had immediately become firm favourites of the staff there. Although both dogs had never met until placed in the same run, the staff assured us that they got on really well, which was just as well really as by sharing a quarantine run the dogs saved the charity some money.

For an 18-month-old pup, the girls at the quarantine were amazed at the size of Beardog. But the important thing was that he was a gentle giant. Hyperactive just like Fubar, he was a handful, but loved his cuddles: he would stand on his back legs and drape his lanky front paws over the girls' shoulders.

We would have to find a home for Beardog eventually, but I had six months to do that so I relaxed a little as I concentrated on the up-and-coming test we were about to undergo.

The preparations for the Crufts show had kept getting more and more demanding and, a fortnight or so before we were due to head up to the NEC, the organisers let us know that the BBC needed to film a short, five-minute clip of me and Lisa in which we introduced the dogs, and briefly told their story.

I knew immediately that this wasn't going to be as easy as it sounded. We weren't members of the public who could just stand in front of the cameras and chat away merrily. Because we were in the Armed Forces, both of us would have to seek permission from our relevant press offices. This didn't exactly fill us with optimism, for more than one reason.

First of all, what I had done back in Afghanistan had, strictly speaking, been a breach of my orders. When I had first set up a simple run and kennel for Nowzad, my boss had turned a blind eye. But, after a while, he'd had to give me an official talking-to. I had at one point specifically been told that I couldn't rescue and keep the dogs. I had chosen to ignore the order; never the smartest of moves.

I had got away with it in Afghanistan but, back here in the UK, I had got the distinct feeling that the higher command weren't really that interested in my forthcoming appearance at a dog show. Neither Lisa nor I had really got a positive vibe from the military machine over our continued involvement with the charity. It was frustrating and we were worried it would affect the decision allowing us to be filmed.

The biggest reason for our pessimism, however, was the fact that the BBC wanted to bring their camera crew into the military base where I was serving. It was a top-level security establishment and, in the present climate, an obvious target for terrorists and bad guys. Anyone trying to visit the place had to first be invited, and then secondly pass through the tough security checks to get past the heavily armed marines at the security gate. I could easily see that not happening if a BBC crew turned up asking to shoot footage of a marine and his Afghan dogs.

This was too good an opportunity to miss, however, so I had to at least try to get permission to do the filming. I sat down in front of the computer and crafted an email explaining my cause and how it would benefit the reputation of the Marines. As I sent it off to the powers-that-be,

I did the only thing left that would help us – I firmly crossed my fingers.

I was pleasantly surprised by the response. The public relations officials of the Marines gave us the green light. And the camera crew didn't lose any time once I had confirmed we could go ahead with the shoot: they wanted to come the very next day.

'Lisa, we're filming tomorrow,' I informed her by mobile phone, after the twentieth time of waiting for her to pick up.

'Crap, I haven't got permission yet, let alone the time off,' she replied, suddenly in a flap.

'Best get on the case then, honey, otherwise I'm going to be a TV star without you,' I said, deliberately winding her up.

'No, Nowzad is going to be the star. You'll just be the dumb-ass on the other end of the lead,' she replied, giggling.

Twenty-four hours later, the large lens of a camera was following me as I led Nowzad and Tali across the Commandant General's Court Parade. We were inside the hallowed home of all Royal Marines, the Commando training centre.

I felt extremely self-conscious and exposed, and I could only imagine the ribbing I would take from any colleagues who saw me.

As the camera crew gave me directions, I tried to look

everywhere I could except at one particular window. We had been criss-crossing the Court for several minutes and I couldn't understand why I had not seen them before.

Well, there was nothing I could do now; it was too late.

As Lisa and I turned again to walk back under the direction of the shoot's director, I couldn't help but turn the clock back 20 years. My mind went back to the day I had stood here, proud as punch in my best dress uniform, as I had passed out of what is known as the hardest infantry training in the world. With my mum and dad either side of me, we had posed for the official military photographer under the gaze of the statue of two bronze Commandos that we were now strolling past as the cameras filmed.

'So much has happened since then,' I thought as we waited patiently for the camera crew to move to a new position. Again.

'Lisa, look at the window to the left of the entry door to Puzzle Palace,' I said through gritted teeth, just in case anybody was watching me. (Puzzle Palace is the name of the building that bordered the Court Parade; it is a maze of dead ends, long identical corridors and hundreds of classrooms spread over three floors. Nobody ever finds the room they want the first time. Nobody.)

'What am I looking for?' Lisa said as we started to walk back across the square for the umpteenth time.

As we turned again, I leant towards her. 'Look in the window, at those two officers standing there. They're the two who banned me from rescuing Nowzad.' One had been the commanding officer of the unit I had served with and the other officer had been the second in command. Both had directed that the order banning the keeping of 'feral animals' be enforced. Thankfully Now Zad had been too much of a remote location for them to find out if their orders were being obeyed and besides I had assumed that they had more important matters to concentrate their efforts on.

I knew the two officers had both been promoted and moved on since we had returned from Afghanistan, but I hadn't realised to an office overlooking the square I was now being filmed in until I saw them both standing there looking out at me.

'Oh, yes, I see,' Lisa exclaimed as she caught on to what I meant. 'That's you in the shit, then.'

'Well, they can't send the dogs back,' I said as we stopped again while we waited for the TV crew to lift and shift into a new position, to take seemingly the same footage from a different angle. I was sure they had already filmed from there before. How much film did they need of the four of us crossing the same courtyard?

'But I suppose they could send me,' I suddenly realised, hoping they weren't currently hatching that very plot.

Secretly, I was actually hoping that it was winding the two officers up nicely as we paraded up and down.

'Oh, to be a fly on the wall of that office right now,' I said to Lisa out of the corner of my mouth, all the while smiling heartily for the camera.

*

With Crufts now less than a week away, life seemed to have sped up even more. And as if preparing Nowzad and Tali for their big moment wasn't taxing enough, the charity had become even more of an emotional rollercoaster ride than usual.

It had been the fate of Blue that had been exercising my mind the most.

My initial concerns about Blue's health had turned out to be well-founded. In the wake of making contact with the soldier, I had received a steady flow of emails both from him and Koshan. They didn't paint a happy picture.

The soldier told me that Blue had gone off his food, had become lethargic and the lesions around his eyes and nose were becoming worse.

Blue was the first dog we had been contacted about that had medical problems, so we had been lucky in that respect. There was little I could do from the UK, so I sent a long email to Koshan describing Blue's symptoms as best I could. He was hugely experienced with sickly dogs and also had occasional access to a vet at the centre.

It hadn't taken him long to get back to me. Unfortunately, the symptoms were all too familiar to him. He was fairly certain that Blue had canine leishmaniasis.

Leishmaniasis is caused by the leishmania parasite, a nasty little bastard that is passed on by the bite of the phlebotomine sand fly. After Googling it and doing research, it was obvious that this was a nasty and extremely dangerous condition. I also discovered that the location of the base in which the soldier was operating was a leishmaniasis hotspot.

The diagnosis certainly clarified things, for me at least. Leishmaniasis is fatal unless treated early with the right drugs. It could also be transmitted to humans.

I typed an email to the soldier. I was blunt and to the point. I explained Koshan's diagnosis and what it meant. Blue had to be transported to the Afghan rescue centre as soon as he could arrange it.

The news seemed to galvanise the soldier. Within two days he'd got back to me with some hopeful news. An Afghan driver had agreed to transport Blue – for a small fee – to the rescue centre.

I spent the next couple of days obsessively checking my email for updates. And, sure enough, three days after Blue had set off, Koshan sent me a short but sweet note confirming he had made it safely. The even better news was that one of the few vets practising in Afghanistan would be visiting the shelter the very next day.

It seemed like we'd struck lucky.

Having been the bearer of bad news before, I felt a huge sense of relief as I emailed both the soldier and his mother to let them know that Blue was safe, for the time being at least.

CHAPTER NINE

Operation Hilton

'Come on, come on, pick up,' I whispered urgently once again at the brightly back-lit screen of my mobile, willing the person I was dialling to answer with the simple power of thought.

'Well?' Lisa asked anxiously from behind me, using her free hand to prod me in the back.

'Wait, it's still ringing.'

'Where the hell is she?' Lisa asked again.

Along with Nowzad and Tali, Lisa and I were standing in the dark shadows of the thick shrubbery outside the rather grand entrance of the Hilton hotel at the National Exhibition Centre in Birmingham, trying hard not to be spotted.

Our camouflage was far from perfect. The light spilling from the windows opposite us was just bright enough to outline Lisa and Tali clearly.

Nowzad was by my side, waiting patiently, too, for the signal to go. I was sure the little bugger had just had a wee on my shoe, but I couldn't be sure. Before I could look down to explore my phone burst into life.

'Hi, Pen, sorry. I got distracted at the bar,' a bubbly female voice said.

'Lucy, this is no time for socialising: this is a mission and lives could be at stake,' I countered, trying to sound as serious as I could.

'Oh, yeah, sorry,' came the sheepish reply.

Lucy was married to a Royal Naval officer and had read about the exploits of Nowzad in the local naval press. Working as a sales representative for a major dog food company who were exhibiting at Crufts, she had immediately offered her services. Coincidentally, the company that she represented was also putting her up in the Hilton, so Lucy had been well up for some cloak and dagger stuff when I had asked for her help.

Maybe I had over-exaggerated the 'lives at stake' bit, but this was a carefully planned operation. With Lucy as our advance guard, we had to guide the dogs through the hotel reception without any incident. Either that or Lisa, Nowzad and Tali and I were sleeping in the van that night.

'So is the reception clear?' I asked, holding a hand up to Lisa to cut off the already-forming questions.

'Well, it's as good as it's going to get, I reckon,' Lucy replied.

'Right, it's now or never, get the lift ready,' I said before hanging up.

'We are a go,' I said to Lisa, summoning up as much

military authority as I could muster. I gripped Nowzad's lead even tighter.

'Lisa, are you ready?' I asked as I checked the entrance to the building was clear once more.

'Ready,' came the reply from the darkness behind me.

Suddenly, a little old lady, dressed in a heavy dark over-coat, exited the building. A rotund little Pug, forced into wearing a ridiculous-looking pink doggie coat complete with studs, was desperately scurrying along to keep up with her.

Letting Nowzad run headlong into the lady and her ankle-biter would not have been good.

'One second,' I said.

As I watched the odd couple disappearing from view, I found my mind wandering. How on earth had I got myself into this ridiculous situation?

The reason for this caution was that Crufts organisers had arranged for us to have a room for two nights at the Hilton hotel, which was about half a mile from the gigantic exhibition halls that would be hosting Crufts and the finals night. As Lisa and I couldn't really afford one night at the Hilton, let alone two, we were rather looking forward to somebody else paying.

Fizz Dog and Beamer Boy were staying with Lisa's parents, but the organisers had got the hotel to agree to Nowzad and Tali staying in the room with us. Presumably they'd been told they were the canine stars of the *Friends for Life* finals. My guess was, however, that they hadn't been told they were two dogs that had, until their release from quarantine just three months earlier, been leading lives as near-feral scavengers. Or that one of them had been a fighting dog to boot. This was why we were being so cautious.

What if Nowzad did have a go at somebody? What if either dog peed on the hotel-room carpet? Or they started howling in the dead of night? The bill we would end up with could bankrupt us. This was the Hilton, after all.

I had spent the past couple of days fretting over the endless possibilities, so had come up with an action plan to cope with all eventualities.

Once inside the hotel room, both dogs would sleep in their canvas fold-up travel crates, which were brilliant bits of kit for the times when we needed to keep the dogs secure for a few hours and, of course, where they would have their comfy dog beds. They would have a large supply of dog chews and treats, too. We'd also make sure to smuggle up some sausages from what was sure to be a very hearty breakfast.

To be extra safe, we were going to leave the dogs in the van during the rehearsals on the Saturday. We'd give them a good long walk beforehand so that they were in the mood for a morning snooze, while we checked out the route and any obstacles we might face on finals night.

We wanted to know what we were going to be up against.

Nowzad and Tali were accustomed to sleeping anywhere; a comfortable dog bed in our insulated van wouldn't even register on their discomfort radar. The alternative – if we left them in the room – didn't bear thinking about. My mind conjured up all sorts of bizarre scenarios. What if both dogs somehow managed to get loose in the hotel room while Lisa and I were at the rehearsals? How much damage could they cause? How would the cleaning staff react when they walked into the room to be confronted by Nowzad? What if, somehow, Nowzad forced his way past the cleaners and ran round the hotel? What if, having terrorised the hotel, he got out into the open and got into the main Crufts arena? Nowzad would become the most feared and infamous dog since the Hound of the Baskervilles.

All of which explained why, after a long walk to stretch out our travel-cramped legs, we were now hiding in the Hilton hotel's bushes, waiting for the all-clear so that we could get Nowzad into our room without any of these doomsday scenarios unfolding.

The plan was simple, formulated after I had carried out a recon op earlier to check out the lay of the land. Having been given the all-clear by Lucy, we would dart out of the bushes and across the car valet point of the lobby of the building, before entering the main reception.

Once inside the hotel, we would take a right out of reception before stopping smartly on our left and hopefully into the lift that would take us to the third floor, where our room was.

I took a deep breath. Lucy should have the lift open and be waiting for us by now.

'Right, *go!*'

As one smooth unit we burst out of the bushes and legged it towards the grand front doors of the Hilton.

'Come on, Nowzad,' I urged as we trotted over the tarmac, his claws making a clip-clop noise as we went. Nowzad already had an eye on one of the supporting posts for the awning that sheltered the entranceway.

'Nowzad, *no*. You can't possibly have any wee left,' I said as I dragged him away.

I grabbed the large brass handle of the front door and quickly glanced through the glass panels. Except for the two receptionists behind the high-fronted desk, the coast seemed clear.

'Go,' I urged Lisa behind me.

I yanked open the door and, like a line backer clearing the way for the quarterback in American football, Lisa moved swiftly ahead of me. I gave her a few yards before I followed with Nowzad tight to my side. I could see Lisa check left towards the bar and then right as we had planned. I followed closely on her heels.

Tali was the easier of the two dogs to control should we be confronted by an approaching show dog. That would give me ample warning to turn Nowzad round and lead him out of the confrontation zone.

I quickly glanced left in the direction of the bar; the assembled crowd of dog people were happily chatting and laughing, oblivious to our entrance.

I couldn't see any dogs. So far, so good.

I had already collected our room key on my solo recon early in the evening, so I followed Lisa as she turned right for the 20-yard dash to the waiting lift across the highly polished floor. Again, the sound of Nowzad's claws made a sharp click-clack sound that seemed very loud to my nervous ears.

As arranged, a grinning Lucy was there, holding the door of the lift. She had half a pint of lager in one hand.

'Cheers, Lucy,' I said as we rushed in and the doors slid shut behind us. We all let out a collective sigh of relief.

I decided some introductions were in order. 'Nowzad, meet Lucy,' I said, somewhat aware of the cramped confines of the lift.

With his lead held tight, Nowzad had no opportunity to lunge at Lucy even if he had wanted to, although to be fair I don't think he did. Lucy owned two large dogs herself and knew not to just throw herself at Nowzad until he had adjusted to her. Besides, I think Nowzad was more interested in being in a lift – as far as we knew it was his first time in one.

Arriving on the third floor, the doors opened on to a deserted corridor but Lucy, still with beer in hand, was dispatched to double-check all was clear, as our room was located past a blind corner in the long bare corridor.

'Looks good,' she yelled back to us. We left the relative safety of the lift and headed quickly in the direction of our room.

Lucy had opened the door and we guided Nowzad and

Tali directly into the travel crates that we'd readied in advance. Both dogs could immediately smell the dog chews inside. Without a second glance they disappeared into the depths of the comfy dens.

'Good job, team!' I said as we high-fived each other.

'And Lisa, this is Lucy by the way.' I introduced the two girls to each other for the first time. Well, Nowzad had to be first, didn't he?

'Hi, Lisa,' Lucy said as they shook hands. 'What's all the fuss about Nowzad?' she asked. 'He seems a right softie.'

Lisa smiled. 'Only when he wants to be, Lucy, only when he wants to be,' came her long-suffering reply. It seemed Nowzad was becoming successful in his newly acquired art of luring people into a false sense of security.

'You two got time for a bedtime drink?' Lucy asked. 'My company's buying.'

'You read my mind,' I replied as I turned on the giant television screen attached to the room wall. I hoped it would drown out any potential noise if anybody was to stroll past the room. 'There's always time for a beer,' I added. And so, with the two former Afghan strays happily munching away on thick dental chews, we gently closed the hotel room door and headed off to explore the crowded bar.

Amazingly, the morning walk with the dogs round the grounds of the NEC had gone without a hitch. The day was dull and overcast but luckily the weather was fairly mild for early March. There had been very few people milling about in the foyer as we had passed through and thankfully at the back of the hotel we'd even managed to find an open area of rough ground that was completely free of other dog walkers, which was pretty remarkable given it was Crufts weekend.

Both dogs sniffed the ground, keenly following what I imagined were the trails and smells of the local rabbits and foxes that roamed the vast grounds that surrounded the NEC. Afterwards we put the dogs in the van while we had breakfast in the enormous function room; we had reckoned the maid would go into the room at some point to make up the bed and we didn't want to give her a heart attack when she was greeted by Nowzad.

Having eaten like kings, we sneaked a couple of sausages out from the buffet and headed back to the van. The instant Lisa opened the door, the pair of them sprang up in their travel crates, sniffing the air. Nowzad in particular loved sausages and his Afghan nose clocked the smell of the hidden contraband immediately.

'Yes, Nowzad, the sausage is for you,' Lisa called out as she unwrapped them from the red serviettes we'd secreted them in; Nowzad had started to paw the mesh door of his travel crate in his excitement. I broke the sausages into small pieces and buried them under the dry dog food in their bowls, before adding a drop of water to each. Lisa opened the kennels' zip doors just enough to slide the bowls into their confines where, without pausing, both dogs dived into the bowls, hungrily wolfing down food as they searched for the concealed sausage bits. Needless to say they didn't stay hidden for long.

With the dogs happily fed and chilling in the van, we strolled off to meet the *Friends for Life* organising team, along with the four other finalists. Officially it was to be our rehearsal for the live show in the evening, but Lisa and I had decided we would also use the time to suss out the route and any hazards that we might encounter with the dogs later.

We arrived at the NEC halls to find the rest of the finalists gathered round a smartly dressed representative from the Kennel Club. Among the assembled crowd were also several well-behaved dogs that were waiting patiently by the side of their owners. I was relieved we hadn't brought Nowzad and Tali: they would have put me to shame next to these paragons of good manners.

We recognised most of the dogs and their owners from the short video clips that had been playing on the BBC along with ours about Nowzad and Tali. There was Hazel with Connie, the gentle, giant Newfoundland who helped her with household chores after Hazel had damaged her back. Alongside her was Percy the black Labrador, who was wagging his tail eagerly by the side of a young lad, called William, who had been diagnosed with autism. Another lady, Linda, who we also believed had severely injured her back, was happily making a fuss of Sadie, an excitable young German Shepherd. And last but definitely not least, we immediately recognised the bright young figure of Harriet. Harriet suffered from cerebral palsy but hoped with the aid of her adorable, light-tanned Vizsla, Yepa that she would be able to walk again. Her video had shown her swimming with Yepa. It had almost, even I had to admit, brought a tear to my eye. Lisa and I were pretty convinced she would and should win.

We worked our way round the group saying hello, but confused looks greeted us, as heads twisted and turned, looking for the dogs that were meant to be the crucial element of the *Friends for Life* final.

'The dogs are relaxing: they asked if we would come and do the rehearsal for them,' I explained each time.

Under the supervision of the guide, we headed to the main exhibition hall, following the route that would lead us to the main arena later that evening, and our big moment on the telly.

'Oh, shit,' I said as we entered the vast hall.

'Oh, shit too,' Lisa agreed, open-mouthed.

The sight that greeted us was both awe-inspiring and terrifying. The vast halls of the NEC were filled with thousands of dog enthusiasts. It was hardly surprising really, but they were accompanied by hundreds of dogs, each of which seemed to be prancing alongside their owners, undergoing pre-judging in the breed rings or sitting patiently in row after row of what looked to me like airport baggage trolleys. Some dogs were even arranged on specialised grooming tables, where their already immaculately trimmed coats were being given a final cut before the competition began.

And then there was the noise. The sound hit you like a

brick as soon as you entered the enormous space. It was deafening: a mixture of barking dogs, chatting people, impulsive cheering and clapping from around the display rings and, of course, there were constant announcements that boomed and echoed round the halls.

'Oh, this is bad,' I muttered.

Without exception, all of the patiently waiting dogs and their owners of our party seemed oblivious to the racket around them. But to us it sounded horrendous.

'And just how are we going to get the nightmare twins through here?' I nudged Lisa.

'Don't ask me,' Lisa replied. 'It was your smart idea to say yes.'

Even after a few months of training, Nowzad and Tali were still appalling if we crossed paths with any other dogs on our daily walks. It was as if they both assumed the path belonged to them. If another dog approached, Nowzad would still lunge forwards until we had to restrain him by yanking back on his lead and Tali would go into her yelping mode until we dragged the two of them out of sight of the usually well-behaved dog and its unimpressed owner.

What the hell were the two of them going to be like wandering through the packed exhibition halls of the largest dog show on earth?

For a second I wondered if I had been wrong to take part in the show. Maybe it was pushing things for the two Afghan dogs? Perhaps we should think about withdrawing at this stage? Would it be too late to do that?

The group passed by the edge of the commercial stalls that were selling everything that a dog owner could possibly want for their beloved pet: multi-coloured dog beds in all shapes and sizes, flashing dog leads, body harnesses, dog food, and health tablets claiming to cure every canine ailment known. One stall was even selling matching dog outfits and leads.

I pointed them out to Lisa. 'We'd never put Nowzad in one of those,' I exclaimed.

Lisa laughed. 'Yes, I think he'd put up a good fight first if we tried.' She had to shout to be heard above the din.

I spied a stall selling homemade cakes and buns, all meticulously decorated. I was starving. Breakfast had been good but had been nearly two hours ago. As I got close the smell was mouth-watering and I homed in on some gingerbread men.

'How much for two gingerbread men?' I asked.

'Two pounds, love,' came the reply.

I paid and turned to leave, only seconds from dragging a gingerbread man from the bag and giving him the good news as I chewed his head off. It was only then that I noticed the sign: *ALL CAKES ARE HOME BAKED WITH OUR SPECIAL TRIPE RECIPE – ESPECIALLY FOR DOGS.*

I quickly scanned the people milling around me. Thankfully, nobody had been watching as I had been about to eat a tripe baked dog treat.

I casually strolled back over to Lisa before I lost her in the crowd as she turned to catch up with our group.

'What have you bought those for?' Lisa asked, grinning like a Cheshire cat.

'Treats for Nowzad and Tali,' I replied.

'Don't talk rubbish, you were going to eat them,' she said before she burst out laughing.

I playfully slapped her bum as she moved in front of me: 'Honey, I'm not *that* stupid.'

I should have guessed that she would have been watching. Though as my stomach growled, I still wondered what they might taste like.

The rehearsals for that evening were straightforward enough: we were to wait in a holding area outside the main arena until called, and then the four of us were to walk the outside of the ring while the story of Nowzad was broadcast once more.

It suddenly dawned on me that Nowzad might well have flashbacks if he were to see the thousands of spectators packed into the finals ring. It could easily remind him of a dogfight gathering such as he had been a part of back in Afghanistan. All I could hope was that the copious garlic treats I would have with me would reassure him that nothing untoward was going to happen.

With the rehearsal over, we took stock. As we had suspected, the worst part of the evening would be actually getting Nowzad and Tali to the main arena in the first place.

'It will be a nightmare,' I said to Lisa, stating the obvious, as we once more looked with dismay at the hordes of visitors. Every other person had a dog in tow.

'Yeah, it's going to be a nightmare,' was Lisa's only comment.

The organisers wanted to do as many rehearsals as possible. By the end of second run through, both of us felt that we knew the route round the outside of the arena well enough: all we had to do was walk round the outside of the ring before heading to stand in the spot reserved for us at the centre of the arena.

We left those wanting another practice session, in search of a decent cup of tea and a quiet place to discuss our options.

Contrary to our fears, both dogs had been as good as gold along the route from the van and through the exhibition halls to the main arena waiting area.

With our pockets stuffed with garlic treats specially baked for Crufts by Helen, Nowzad and Tali seemed oblivious to the dogs and people that had surrounded and hemmed us in as we made our way to the pre-arranged meeting point.

Thankfully, the crowds in the exhibition halls had thinned considerably from the hordes that had been gathered in the morning, as the evening finals were a ticket holder-only event that had, as always, sold out months ago. Most people had already claimed their seats by the time we walked through with Nowzad and Tali.

My worries of Nowzad lunging at every dog he encountered had been unfounded. As long as I kept feeding him the treats on a regular basis, he was happy walking by my side. Nowzad was still Nowzad, of course, so he still threw in the occasional yank, but that was about it.

'Why aren't the two of them this good at home?' I had said to Lisa as we waited patiently at the back of the queue of finalists as each were introduced in turn and allowed their moment of fame.

Lisa remained sceptical. It wasn't over yet. She just raised her eyebrows at me and continued to distract Tali from a really annoying border collie that was waiting to go in the arena after us to perform a song and dance routine. Its owner obviously was not getting the message that Nowzad and Tali were not the most playful of types.

We had asked to be introduced last so that Nowzad and Tali weren't subjected to too much excitement out in the arena. The noise of the cheering and clapping as the master of ceremonies introduced the next finalist could potentially have scared the pair of them.

I still fully expected something terrible to happen. I had earlier joked to Lisa that because the show was filmed live, Nowzad would probably decide to have a crap in the main arena. The shot would then be played out over and over again on those annoying TVs funniest moments programmes. He'd be famous – but in a really bad way. With this in mind, we had spent nearly two hours walking both dogs around the outside of the hall, allowing Nowzad to wee on everything he could find.

*

'And our last finalist tonight is Sergeant Farthing with his wife, Lisa, and of course, Nowzad and Tali.'

As the MC's introduction boomed round the arena, the darkness that we'd been cloaked in evaporated in an instant. As if on cue, the crowd erupted, cheering and clapping as the spotlight revealed the four of us waiting in the wings. All my nerves disappeared. It was too late to worry now.

I turned to Lisa and smiled. 'Show time.'

We both stepped out into the arena. Any doubts we might have had were irrelevant now. The television cameras were on us and us alone.

The noise from the crowds increased and I smiled down at Nowzad. He really didn't seem that bothered by it at all. He was much more concerned about when the next smelly garlic treat was coming his way. With the glare of the two spotlights tracking our progress, it was impossible to see the thousands of people crammed into the spectator seats of the finals arena watching us. I don't think Nowzad even knew they were there.

Perhaps it was my mind playing tricks on me, but the cheers that greeted Nowzad and Tali seemed to be the loudest of the night. It was a weird feeling. As we made our way round the outside of the ring I glanced up into the darkness, smiling and throwing in a crafty couple of waves to the crowd like I was some over-important pop star.

As we walked, I had to marvel at the absurdity of the situation. Here I was, a serving member of Her Majesty's Armed Forces, running round in front of a huge audience at the biggest dog show in the world with a fighting dog that, until just recently, had lived in one of the most God-forsaken corners of the world. I couldn't help but grin like an idiot. The whole thing was just so bizarre.

As the applause continued to build, I turned to look at Lisa who was also grinning like an idiot as Tali trotted by her side, her long fluffy tail held proudly upright behind her.

We took our places on our designated spotlight and waited while each finalist was presented with a beautiful glass *Friends for Life* trophy as a memento of the evening.

I made a quick strategic decision and urged Lisa forward to accept the award. As she did so, I edged backwards with Nowzad, just in case he decided to have a go at the Chairwoman of the Kennel Club. That really would have ruined his reputation. And the night.

The crowd fell silent as the finals presenter, Matt Baker, waited to announce the winner as voted by the general public. The short video clips of our stories had been aired during every day of Crufts and a public phone vote had been held to decide which dog and owner would win the *Friends for Life* award.

A hush descended as we all waited for the announce-ment. Lisa and I stroked the dogs' heads to reassure them although, truth be told, neither of them seemed the slightest bit bothered by what was going on. There was no doubt: we were far tenser than they were.

'And the winner of the 2008 Kennel Club *Friends for Life*

award as chosen by the British public is …' – Matt paused for effect – 'Harriet and Yepa.'

Once more the crowd erupted as the spotlights around us dimmed and what seemed like every beam in the arena was focused on Harriet.

Together with her dad and, of course, best pal Yepa, who was bouncing up and down like crazy around Harriet, they went forward to collect their well-deserved trophy.

I looked at Lisa and she looked back at me. We both smiled and patted the dogs once more.

'Don't worry, Nowzad; you did well just getting here!' I said into his ear above the noise of the crowd.

I knew that we were both glad that Harriet had won: the 11-year-old and her faithful pal more than deserved the award. I moan like a demon when I have man flu; I didn't even want to imagine how I would cope with something like cerebral palsy. Chatting to Harriet during the day, Lisa and I had both been impressed by her determination to overcome her condition, showing an attitude that most fully able kids her age would do well to adopt.

Nowzad and I could live without being known as the winner of the 2008 final. Besides, I didn't want to imagine the grief I would have got from the lads had I stolen the title from an innocent 11-year-old girl. I was sure I was going to get some grief anyway for being a Royal Marine Commando who had been beaten by an 11-year-old girl.

We were just happy that Nowzad and Tali had had their moment in the spotlight; they hadn't crapped anywhere or tried to eat any other dogs or people. And most importantly of all, our charity had hopefully gained some free publicity. Yeah, we were happy.

As we were ushered out of the ring, we were already focusing on the important task of working out the best route back to the hotel without Nowzad or Tali ruining their 100 per cent good-behaviour record for the evening so far.

Once they had been fed, we were going to have a beer down in the bar and relax ourselves. We had survived Crufts.

It had been a piece of cake, really.

I just hoped Lucy was in the hotel with her company card, as the Hilton bar was bloody expensive.

CHAPTER TEN

Down to Earth

Their 15 minutes of fame seemed to have had no lasting effect on Nowzad or Tali.

Both dogs slept all the way back from Birmingham, slotting straight back into their routine when we got home as if we hadn't been away.

We'd spent so much time worrying about how the whole thing would affect them, but I doubted very much that they had been bothered at all by the events at Crufts. For them, it had just been another day in what was our mad world.

When they got back to the house, they immediately reverted to their old routine. Which meant playing around like six-week-old puppies, something that they never seemed to tire of these days. After the long journey, Nowzad had seemed quite happy to sleep upside down in his bed, his white-haired belly on display. But he wasn't allowed any peace as Tali dived on him again and again to begin one of their play fights.

Interestingly, the dogs' play or interaction was always

the same: both sets of dogs, Nowzad and Tali, and Fizz Dog and Beamer Boy, always seemed to want or need to keep themselves separate, as a pair.

Maybe Nowzad and Tali really didn't speak English.

When he and Tali played now, Nowzad would wriggle and squirm, his black-spotted gums and sparse, yellow-stained teeth on display, taking whatever Tali threw at him. She was like a striking snake that kept recoiling and launching at Nowzad's thickly hair-covered throat, nipping and pinching his skin in thick clumps before deftly jumping out of reach as Nowzad attempted to snap his mouth shut on her muzzle, only to close on thin air. As I sat there watching them, the same thought occurred to me every time I saw them go through this routine: it was a good job they were only playing, otherwise Tali would have been well in the shit.

Beamer Boy eyed them from a distance, itching to get involved, but always wary even when I tried to encourage him over. Old lady Fizz Dog, on the other hand, would sit tall and bark gruffly at their antics, intent on stopping them from playing. As always they had not asked her permission to enjoy themselves.

For me and Lisa, on the other hand, re-entry to real life after Crufts was a bit more of a rude awakening.

We'd got back after a long drive back on the Monday, knowing that work loomed at the crack of dawn the following morning and, sure enough, the minute the alarm went off we were straight back into the routine of juggling the dogs, our day jobs and the ever-growing admin work of the charity. Lisa and I also knew we had to sit down with our diaries and work out which day we were going to squeeze in another ten-hour or so round trip to the quarantine centre to visit Helmand, the only puppy of Tali's to have survived the parvo outbreak at the rescue centre in Afghanistan.

By Tuesday evening the high of the Crufts arena was already a fading memory. And it disappeared completely the minute I clicked on an email from the Afghan centre.

I immediately knew what it was about and really didn't want to open it. Maybe if I didn't then the news wouldn't be real. But I knew it was already too late. It had happened. Blue the Afghan stray that had given so much comfort to the American soldier who had adopted him was dead.

Koshan had sent me an email explaining that Blue's leishmaniasis had been in an advanced stage and untreatable. The rescue centre staff had had no choice but to put Blue to sleep to end his suffering. I just sat and stared at the latest picture of Blue that Koshan had sent me only a few days before we had travelled to Crufts. His big sad puffy eyes stared back at me as he posed for the camera.

It was a hammer blow for me, both personally and for the charity. Blue was the first dog we had failed. And as if that wasn't bad enough, I now had to break the news to an American soldier who was still serving in Afghanistan.

Before doing that, I replied to Koshan and thanked him for everything the rescue staff had done for Blue. It was obvious from his email that he felt that the rescue centre had failed us somehow. But it was obvious that it was not their fault. The lack of facilities and, more importantly, the complete inability to gain access to vaccines and medicines was the reason Blue hadn't survived. Simple as that.

After sending the email to Koshan, I took a minute and began composing an email to the soldier. He was still on the frontline somewhere, but I had no idea where. Blue had meant everything to him and had been a loyal companion through what I knew was a rough tour of duty. The news was going to be hard on him.

I kept it short. But it took me several goes before I had the wording right.

This type of email had not been part of the plan when I had casually decided to form the charity. I had imagined it would all be good-news stories and triumphant home-coming parties.

But not in this case.

I reread the email once more and hit the send button. I stood up and turned the computer off. The rest of the emails could wait. I headed downstairs and joined Lisa in the kitchen, deliberately nudging her as I squeezed past.

'Want a beer?' I asked as I bent down to grab a bottle from the open cupboard by the dogs' water bowl.

Lisa was chopping potatoes for the evening meal and threw me a quizzical look.

'It's a bit early, isn't it? And it's only Tuesday,' she said.

'Yeah, I know,' I replied as I reached for the bottle opener. 'But Blue didn't make it.'

Lisa stopped chopping and turned to face me. I handed her the opened bottle and reached for another one. Suddenly, I knew we didn't feel hungry any more. Instead we walked into the living room and made a fuss of our pack who were sprawled out on the floor. Neither of us said anything. We didn't need to.

The summer evening was gorgeous, the cloudless sky a deepening blue as I looked towards the hills to the west. The heat stuck to me like glue even though my watch said it was after six. As the pack had already been walked, I should have been throwing my climbing shoes and chalk bag into my van and heading off to the moor for an evening's bouldering.

Working out the moves while climbing over the cool granite tors of Dartmoor had been all I dreamed of when I had sat for countless dull hours on watch, in that other world that was the Afghanistan solution.

But right now I just felt mentally drained.

Instead I grabbed a couple of cold beers out of the fridge and plonked myself down in a pink fold-up sun chair we used for relaxing in the back garden. Obviously, I had not had a say in the choice of colour.

The charity computer hadn't even been turned on, and it wasn't going to be, either, even though I knew there would be several emails that would all state they needed immediate responses.

It was a lovely summer's evening and for once I was having some time to myself.

The dogs were equally laid back. Fizz Dog was stretched out on the grass while Nowzad and Beamer Boy were hiding from the heat in the cool confines of the kitchen, both splayed out and panting heavily on the tiled floor. Only Tali had come to sit with me. As I lay there soaking up the last rays of the evening sun, sipping my beer, I stroked her head with my free hand.

Placing the bottle on the ground between my feet, I was amused to see that Tali, after a tentative investigation of the beer's smell, turned her nose up with an 'I don't think so' gesture before quickly trotting off into the house.

'Beamer Boy wouldn't have been so fussy!' I called after her.

Beamer Boy loved the taste of beer, as both Lisa and I had discovered to our horror while relaxing in a pub beer garden one evening after a long dog walk round Glastonbury Tor. He had slurped the last two mouthfuls from a pint that I had unwittingly just placed down beside me and ever since then, all beer glasses left lying around him were fair game. Several of our unsuspecting friends had been caught out when they'd unwittingly left a pint glass within reach of Beamer Boy's tongue.

I was going to make no such mistake today. Ever the prepared marine, I had brought with me from the fridge two more bottles of beer and, of course, the bottle opener. They were all staying safely in my lap.

My brain focused on absolutely nothing as I drank the beer with my eyes closed, the fading heat of the sun on my face. 'I could get used to this,' I thought. It was easy to cast my mind back to the dusty surroundings of the Afghan compound that had been our home – I could picture the yellowish-brown mud that everything was built from as if I had been there only yesterday.

Back in Helmand, just as I was doing now, I had spent my downtime sat amongst the Nowzad pack, the fading Afghan sun washing over me, trying its best to keep us warm before the onslaught of the freezing Afghan winter night arrived.

Admittedly we hadn't had beer to drink, just a hastily made cup of tea from the makeshift galley while the chef had been looking the other way. But Nowzad had been just the ticket to take my mind off the constant feeling of danger that lurked behind every corner when we ventured outside the walls.

Now though it wasn't fear that I worried about. It was stress of a different kind. The mounting paperwork and politics at work felt like they could drive me to despair at times and the calmness I felt from being surrounded by Nowzad and the pack brought me back down to earth.

Three or four bottles later, the dogs were fed and I was sitting on the sofa with two more bottles lined up, ready for the start of my *Battlestar Galactica* DVD box set.

Lisa was on Dartmoor supervising the latest entry of naval recruits as they undertook what the Navy called a 'remote and wild expedition' that was vital to their young recruits' development (but to us marines was known as a camping trip), so I knew now was the time to watch my DVD in peace. Lisa didn't get science fiction and would annoy me constantly, usually by ringing her mother for a chat whilst sitting in the living room next to me.

Across the estuary to the south, two or three miles distance, an outdoor rock concert was in full flow. I had read somewhere that eighties pop legends *Ultravox* were playing and, sure enough, I could make out the strains of 'Vienna' floating across on the perfect summer evening air.

As I settled down to the DVD, I closed the back door to block out the unwanted music. By now all the dogs would be in their beds anyway.

Soon I was lost in a world of lasers and spaceships, strange aliens and bad guys as, for once, I did nothing. All thoughts of who I was going to hassle next for money to get 30 marines away skiing at the start of the winter were forgotten.

The sudden flinch of Nowzad's head followed by the twitching of what was left of his ears made me momentarily turn away from the film. He sat up, his eyes fixed on the living room window.

'What's up, Nowzad?' I asked, as I kept one eye on the film and the other on him.

He had that look I knew well. The scared, silly look – the one where he wasn't happy, at all.

Suddenly I could hear fireworks exploding in the skies above the estuary.

'It's just the end of the concert, I imagine,' I said to Nowzad.

Sure enough, when I stood up and looked through the gap in the drawn curtains, I saw an array of exploding rockets that signalled the finale of the concert. I turned the volume on the telly up to drown out the noise and stroked Nowzad's head.

'It's okay, buddy, the fireworks are a long way off this time,' I reassured him as he settled back down. 'You're not going to have to live through New Year's Eve again.'

I returned to the sofa and fell back into the world of outer space. But within two minutes I was interrupted, this time by Beamer Boy barking and running into the living room, before turning tail and zooming off back down the hall. It was as if he was panicking about something, which was totally out of character.

The movie was coming to a crucial point. The bad guy was about to explain his master plan of evil to the captured hero of the series.

'Beamer Boy, shut up,' I scolded him. 'It's just fireworks.'

Admittedly they were sounding louder so I turned the telly up a bit more.

But Beamer Boy didn't stop. He continued barking and running in and out of the room.

'Beamer Boy, will you please shut up?' I shouted as I put my half-finished beer down and stood up.

But he didn't listen. Instead, he gave another short volley of barks before charging down the hall yet again.

'What are you going on about, Beamer Boy?' I called after him as I went to investigate, suddenly curious, the bad guy's evil plot momentarily forgotten. I glanced at Nowzad curled in his bed, the noise from the TV drowning out the end of the fireworks display.

As I entered the hall at pace, I immediately clocked that Fizz Dog was curled up tightly in her bed too, totally oblivious to the racket that her buddy Beamer Boy was making.

'Oh, shit.'

I stopped dead in my tracks.

Tali always slept by the front door on her oversized brown comfy dog bed. Except, Tali wasn't asleep on her oversized brown comfy dog bed. She was nowhere to be seen.

My heart raced as I turned and looked at Beamer Boy as he sprinted out of the kitchen and back towards where I was standing motionless in the hall, all the while barking at me for what seemed like the thousandth time.

My chilled-out evening exploded into a million fragments as my heart went into overdrive. The realisation hit me like a sledgehammer. I had locked Tali outside.

I bolted towards the back door as my heart leapt into my mouth. As the fireworks exploded in the sky outside, the shape of Tali desperately attacking the back door, impossibly trying to break through the plastic panelling to get to the safety of inside, was clearly visible. Her desperate whines for help had gone unheard except for Beamer Boy, and I had continually ignored him.

I wrenched the door open and Tali shot past my legs and down the hall. The sudden flares of the fireworks lighting up the sky in brilliant blues and reds redoubled in intensity as the organisers went all-out to impress the crowd. But they didn't impress me.

The mental trauma that I had put Tali through was all I could think about. Tali had been stranded outside with nowhere to hide during the onslaught of the entire display.

I slammed the back door shut and went to find her.

'Thanks buddy. Sorry I didn't listen,' I said hurriedly to Beamer Boy as I stopped to pat his head.

I quickly set off down the hallway and into the living room after Tali. Just as she had done on New Year's Eve, she had hidden herself under the coffee table, desperately crawling round and round in circles as if she was trying to dig herself into the ground.

I quickly knelt down so I could get my head and arm under the table.

'Sorry, sorry, Tali,' I repeated, as I stroked and stroked to soothe her.

Why the hell hadn't I realised? What a fucking idiot. Tali's little white-haired body was shaking like crazy. Her normally inquisitive, gentle eyes were wide with fright and she was letting out little quiet whining noises. The once-impending end of the universe was forgotten as the DVD played irrelevantly on the TV behind me, but I didn't register the noise.

'Shhh, it's okay, Tali. I'm so sorry, little lady,' I whispered softly as I tried slowly to drag her body towards me. The table was too narrow for me to get any more than my head and neck under it, but when we were close enough so that my head could touch hers, I pulled her in tight to me.

Why hadn't I bloody checked to see what Beamer Boy was barking at?

'Sorry, sorry, Tali,' I whispered again, as reassuringly as I could, while I mentally scolded myself for not realising she had been left outside.

It was over an hour before she stopped shaking and I could leave her curled up in her bed by the front door.

CHAPTER ELEVEN

Down on the Farm

The familiar fields of the rolling Wiltshire countryside slipped past the van window as I drove down the country lane. Normally, I would have been annoyed to be stuck behind a lumbering tractor whose driver, I was sure, was taking great pleasure in engaging the go-slow gear. As I tooted my horn at him to try and encourage him to go a little faster as he trundled along the hedgerow-enclosed lane, I could see from his rear-view mirror that he was laughing at me.

That was my father-in-law for you.

In truth, I was happy moving along at a leisurely pace. It made it easier for me to look occasionally over my shoulder at the still-trembling passenger in the back seat. Apart from the brown patches that ran the entire length of his skinny frame, the little dog was a spit of his mum, Tali. Little Helmand was even sitting exactly as she had done when she'd travelled in the van along these same lanes.

I imagined the confused young pup had no idea what

was going on. Throughout the journey, I had been trying to reassure him about what was about to happen but, of course, he didn't understand me. I just hoped he would pick up on the tone of my voice.

As the middle of July approached it was a relief to be heading back from the quarantine kennels for the last time: for the foreseeable future at least. The ten-hour drive up and down the motorways to see Helmand during his six-month stay had been a drain on my time and energy. But he'd had a great time there, of course.

Within weeks of his arrival in quarantine, Helmand had found his voice and become the darling of the quarantine. It soon dawned on all concerned that he was the spit of Tali, with his go-faster legs and ears that swirled like radars, picking up the slightest sound from miles away.

And he liked birds, too. The staff regaled us with tales of how he would sit for hours watching the birds flutter round the branches of the trees that stood outside his quarantine kennel.

In the later months, he had also become a firm favourite with other visitors to the quarantine, many of whom sneaked in to spend five minutes with Helmand after playing with their own dogs.

But it was now time for him to adjust to his new life and his new owners: Lisa's mum and dad.

'Here we go, Helmand. This is going to be your new home, buddy,' I said as we finally turned into the farmyard. 'You won't go short of a few walks here.'

That was certainly true. Brian, my father-in-law, was an early bird. By six o'clock each morning he was out and about, walking the fields with his dogs. He learned from us, however, that not all dogs were as controllable as his own.

It still brought a smile to my face to remember the time he had first taken Fizz Dog for a walk. We had taken Fizz Dog down to the farm while both of us were away on extended duty. As dog owners, Lisa's parents had offered to do the dog-sitting for us, and we were really grateful for the offer as we would have had to have paid for kennels.

One particular afternoon, after Brian had finished feeding the cows, he had unwittingly decided that Fizz Dog could do no harm if let off the lead in the middle of one of the sizeable ploughed fields that he was walking across with his two dogs, Lily and Bramble. He had realised the second he had unclipped Fizz Dog from the lead that it was a big mistake.

Fizz Dog had seen a young fawn grazing two fields away from the one they were all standing in. Before Brian could react, she had shot away.

Brian used to be fairly fit as he spent many years turning out for the local football team, but he quickly realised he was no match for the gazelle-like Rottie as she charged off in the direction of the unsuspecting deer. Added to this, the fields on the farm were surrounded by tall prickly hedge-rows, the sort you wouldn't want to try and barge through unless wearing a suit of armour. While Fizz Dog managed to duck low underneath the hedges seemingly without breaking stride, Brian was forced to throw himself through the barbed wire-like branches as he fought to get into the next open field.

He had finally caught up with Fizz Dog two fields later, where she was sitting, panting heavily, the young fawn nowhere to be seen. Brian was blowing even harder but the worst damage was to his new walking jacket. It had been badly torn and ripped by the hedges. And he had never let us forget it.

I pulled over next to the grain silo, slid out of the van and walked round to the side door.

Brian had parked the tractor and walked over to join us.

'Okay, Brian, ready to meet Helmand?' I asked. He nodded.

Marlene, my mother-in-law, had been up to meet Helmand during his quarantine but the commitments of the farm had prevented Brian from making the journey. I slid open the door and grabbed Helmand by his harness as he made a leap for freedom. 'Not so fast, little one.'

Helmand was still wary of all strangers. Although popular, he had been a nightmare at the quarantine centre, darting from one corner of his pen to the other to avoid the clutches of the girls, especially during the early days after his arrival. It had taken until the last couple of months in quarantine for him to relax enough to consider approaching a visitor for treats and cuddles.

So it was no real surprise that as Brian reached down

to say hello, Helmand shot backwards, pulling against the lead.

'Don't worry about it, Brian. It'll probably take a while,' I reassured him, not that he looked worried in the least. Both he and Marlene knew that Helmand was going to be a bit of a handful at the start. And they, more than anyone, knew that looking after any Afghan stray wasn't going to be an easy ride. After all, they had seen us with Nowzad.

'Come on, Helmand,' Brian said, as Helmand eventually relaxed. 'Let's go and meet Lily.'

With a firm grasp on his lead, Brian let Helmand trot round the mud-covered farmyard. A batch of young heifers, due soon to be released into the fields and the attention of the resident bull, stood casually eyeing the new arrival. Helmand barked at them and carried on dragging Brian round the edge of the hard standing. But progress was slow as he was doing the usual Afghan dog trick of sniffing everything he could.

'Come on, Helmand, you've got to meet your new buddy.'

Lily the Labrador was the oldest of our families' dogs. When I had first met Lisa and been introduced to her parents, Lily had been a wide-eyed young Labrador pup sitting in their laps, her long, plumed tail wagging excitedly as everyone made a fuss of her. She loved water and especially loved rolling in crap, much to the dismay of the in-laws, both things obviously being in abundance on the farm. She got on really well with Fizz Dog and Beamer Boy whenever they visited the farm, and loved nothing more than racing to the van so she could join them for a drive. She'd sit there as happy as Larry, watching the world go by from the comfort of the back seat.

We both walked Helmand over to the wooden gate that led into the back garden of the farm house. Lily was already enthusiastically pressing her brown snout through the gaps so she could get a glimpse of the new arrival.

'Hi, Lily, this is Helmand,' I called over to her as we approached. I could see her big brown tail waving madly above the top of the gate even if I couldn't actually see *her*.

Brian opened the gate and we were pulled into the garden as Lily bounded after Helmand who, still attached to Brian by his lead, had raced up the garden path. Just like his mum, Helmand was quick off the mark and Brian had to move fast to keep up with him.

Helmand stopped, turned and stood stock-still as Lily cautiously moved in closer to say hello. Lily thought every person and every dog was her friend, and her tail confirmed this as it was wagging like crazy as she moved to greet the youngster. For a second both dogs rubbed noses and exchanged hellos.

Clearly satisfied with the brief meeting, Helmand turned tail, dragging Brian with him as he scurried off to explore the rest of the garden.

I hadn't brought Tali with me as she is not the greatest fan of long journeys. Besides, I thought the excitement of meeting Lily and getting used to his new surroundings would be enough for the Afghan youngster. Introducing his mum into the equation was probably not a great idea. Seeing him running round, though, there was no doubt in my mind that Helmand was a real chip off the old block. I could see that Brian was going to have his hands full, stopping the pup from running off.

'Probably not a good idea to let him off the lead for a while, Brian,' I said as Helmand finished touring the garden and returned to where I was standing, making a fuss of Lily.

'Not bloody likely,' came Brian's reply. 'I still haven't sewn my jacket up from Fizz Dog's little escapade.'

I smiled as Brian continued to walk Helmand round the yard. The little one was still sniffing at everything and anything in his path. But he seemed relaxed. He was doing okay really, all things considered.

For a moment I took in the view and looked out across the fields, down towards the lone oak tree that dominated the centre of the adjacent field. As I did so, I couldn't help but feel good. The charity was beginning to make a difference. We had had some great results.

Only the day before, I had sat chuckling to myself as I read the email that had flashed up on my computer screen. It had been from Dorothy, the mother of Chris, the Dutch marine who had adopted Fubar.

I always knew when an email was from Dorothy as the subject title was always the same: 'The Afghan Princess.'

From some of the photos she'd sent me of the young dog sitting regally on the carpet in her living room, it seemed entirely fitting.

It had been several weeks now since Fubar had been flown to Holland. She had grown quickly in quarantine and was now almost unrecognisable from the vulnerable pup that had almost been crushed by an armoured vehicle.

In one of the first of her regular emails, Dorothy had described how Fubar's strong Afghan tail could be heard banging excitedly against the inside of the travel crate as she had passed through Dutch customs. Safely through, she had been met by an overjoyed Chris.

Chris was now safely back at the Dutch marine base, but already his unit was training to go back to Afghanistan again. Thanks to his friends and family, however, a fantastic support network was already in place, looking after Fubar. Chris's charming girlfriend was on hand to take daily charge and if she was busy then Dorothy would take over the duties.

Dorothy and Chris regularly kept us up to date on Fubar's progress. We learned that she had generated a lot of interest from Dutch television on her arrival 'home', even to the point that Dutch dog food company Energique had offered her free food for life. With four canine mouths to feed, we would have been glad for some of that action! We also heard that Fubar had been trained to behave pretty well for a canine Afghan refugee. She thoroughly enjoyed being taken for long walks round the local parks, followed by lazy afternoons lounging in the comfort of the family home. And, just like Nowzad, Fubar was instinctively protective of her family 'pack' and would leap up barking at any noise that wasn't a familiar part of her daily world.

But she was very different from Nowzad in other ways, probably because Chris had taken her in as a young pup. Dorothy told me that Fubar had the ability to recognise her name and apparently would come happily running back 99.9 per cent of the time. How we would have loved that luxury with either Nowzad or Tali! We would have to be in the middle of nowhere for that to happen and even then probably only Nowzad would be given the freedom to try. Tali had to be forever under the control of a lead. Where she was concerned, the idea of recall was but a dream.

Dorothy's latest update contained a brilliant story. She had been out that day for her regular walk with Fubar. As they'd strolled around the local park, Dorothy had let Fubar off the lead to gallop free as she loved to do. As always she had been instantly distracted by the many smells of the flower beds and hedgerows and had headed off to explore. Dorothy described how the wayward Afghan stray would lift her head, check on the whereabouts of her human guardian and make a half-hearted attempt to trot back in her direction, before being waylaid once more by the latest smell to hit her nostrils.

'Fubar, Fubar,' Dorothy had called, raising her voice to be heard.

As she watched the zigzagging Fubar, Dorothy noticed a sprightly old lady approaching purposefully.

The old lady had been watching the antics of the playful dog and was smiling broadly.

'Fubar, that's a lovely name,' she said.

Without really knowing what else to say, Dorothy had agreed with her. There was no way she could have expected the old lady's next comment, and nearly choked once she was sure she had heard correctly.

'Yes, it is really nice,' the old lady had continued. 'I wish I had been named Fubar.' She then headed off, still smiling happily.

I giggled again as I reread the email. We actually had to be careful when we ran fund-raising efforts for the Afghan dogs as, on several occasions when I told Fubar's story, people had asked me what her name meant. Each time I had ducked the question.

I still couldn't believe that Chris had given his dog that name. And I could believe even less that little old ladies in parks in Holland were shouting it or, even worse, wishing they'd been christened Fubar, too.

With the day drawing on, I decided that it was time I left Brian, Lily and Helmand to get properly acquainted. It had already been a long day and the journey home was at least another three hours along the congested motorways of the south west.

As I drove home making mental lists of all the things

that had to be done, I started to seriously wonder how we were going to keep pace with the speed at which the charity was evolving. With our demanding day jobs, owning four energetic dogs and trying to have a life, we were seriously running out of hours in the day.

Something had to give.

CHAPTER TWELVE

The Weak Link

'Okay, that hurts,' I mumbled to myself as the pain shot up my spine then down again, and into my right butt cheek, where it promptly did a U-turn and charged straight back the way it had come.

I can't have been a pretty sight. I was lying face down with my nose pressed against the dirt-stained carpet of my office on the base. All I could see in front of me was the front of the lower filing cabinet drawer that I had just bent down to open.

The spasm of pain I had felt in my back as I had pulled the drawer open had sent me crashing to the floor. Luckily my hands had caught my fall and I had lowered myself to the ground in a hastily collapsing push-up. The problem now was I couldn't actually get back up again. Whenever I attempted to move my body upwards the shooting pain firing down my back was unbearable. Even for a marine.

I tried to roll over but I didn't even have the strength to do that. My back was completely locked in the position I had fallen in.

'Bugger,' I mumbled aloud again. There was nothing for it. I was going to have to shout for help. 'Anybody fancy giving me a hand?' I said, raising my voice. Andy who normally worked at the desk opposite me was away for the day, so my hope was that the boss or the wing sergeant major might hear me.

I hadn't expected the sound of urgent footsteps or voices of concern, but the piss-taking was instantaneous: 'Colour Sergeant Farthing, the Corps does not pay you to lie on the floor all day. Any chance you want to get back to work?' the boss's voice called over.

I couldn't actually see him as I was facing the wrong way, but I was pretty sure he was trying not to laugh.

'Boss, in a bit of pain here, could do with some help,' I said in short bursts between gritted teeth.

'Sergeant Major, I may need a hand here,' the boss, a major, yelled towards the next office down the hallway.

More footsteps and I soon knew the sergeant major was now alongside the boss.

'Pen, what *are* you doing? Lisa keeping you that busy at night, is she?'

As with all things military, unless it is a life-or-death situation, the lads will find a funny side to it. Bring it on, I thought. I knew it was only going to get worse. And the temptation to join in the laughter was only tempered by the fact that I knew it would be extremely painful. Any kind of movement seemed to induce a shooting pain.

Soon the office was a hub of laughing and mickey-taking

physical-training instructors, none of whom had actually done anything to help me get up. I was still staring at the half-open filing cabinet drawer.

'As much as I hate to disturb your fun and games, could somebody *please* help me get *up*,' I yelled after what seemed like five minutes of being stepped over and around as people knelt to prod and poke me while making predictable jokes about getting old and lying down on the job.

Finally I was hauled up and, with little regard for my comfort, carried across to the base sick bay. Every step was an exercise in seeing if the pain could get any worse. Apparently it could. But my muffled screams were only rewarded with more piss-taking.

After what seemed like a 10-mile hike, I was dumped on an examination table in agony. Thankfully, a couple of injections directly into the muscles around my lower spine soon eased the pain.

I asked someone to give Lisa a call and then waited patiently while she left work to collect me. Thankfully, she'd brought our van so I was able to lie flat on my back for the journey home. I felt every bump in the road.

Lisa, too, seemed to have been overcome with the desire to laugh at my predicament. As I struggled to get on my feet when we arrived home she couldn't resist making jokes about how a navy PTI was helping a marine PTI.

'Ho ho, honey,' I grimaced at her. 'But, by the way, I haven't tried to go to the toilet yet; I may need some help.'

Which was a thought that quickly wiped the smile off Lisa's face as she helped me hobble into the house.

'Not good, Colours,' the naval medical surgeon said matter of factly as he viewed the digital image of the MRI scans of my back. 'Not good at all.'

He was stating the blindingly obvious. It was now nearly two weeks since I had collapsed when opening the filing cabinet and I was still hobbling around. I looked more like Golum from *The Lord of the Rings* than a senior PTI in Her Majesty's elite Royal Marine Commandos. I bloody knew it wasn't good.

'No more running for you, I'm afraid,' the surgeon continued, as he studied the scans more closely.

'Sir, what do you mean no more running?' I asked.

I had been for a run nearly every day since I was 15 years old. I loved running. And I was a Royal Marine, for Christ's sake. When we went running we went on for ever.

'Well, to put it simply, you have advanced degenerative disease of your lower spine. Three of your lower discs are severely compressed. They won't get better, only worse,' he said.

I loved the straight talk. No softly softly approaches here. Just straight to the point. And apparently I was screwed.

The surgeon gave me a mildly sympathetic look then closed the images down, the computer screen reverting to the screensaver image of the Commando dagger.

'How long have you got left?' he asked, sitting back in his chair and looking at me.

'What, in the Marines, you mean?' I asked just to be sure I hadn't missed something even more serious.

He nodded.

'Another two and a half years,' I replied.

Again, his response was unsubtle and straight to the point.

'No, you don't,' he said, at which point I thought, 'He's enjoying this.'

'Colour Sergeant Farthing,' he continued, 'I'm recommending that you attend a medical board as soon as possible.'

I was in this predicament because I had bent down to open a filing cabinet. I had spent the last two weeks on sick leave at home and had spent most of the time flat on my back, not because I wanted to be there but because getting up or sitting down was a physical feat of endurance that drained every ounce of my energy. It took all my composure to stop myself from screaming if my back twisted even the tiniest amount.

In the mornings, Lisa would help me negotiate the stairs before leaving me lying on the living-room floor with the TV remote control in one hand, surrounded by Nowzad, Tali, Beamer Boy and Fizz Dog, who all decided to help by plonking themselves down next to me.

Thankfully, Lisa was able to give them all a walk before

she headed off to work. But for the rest of the day they, too, were confined to the living room with me, until I could pluck up the strength to push myself up on to all fours, before using the sofa to prop myself into a sort of hunched standing position. The high-strength painkillers didn't seem to be doing a thing.

Nowzad and Tali really did not seem that bothered by the enforced rest, but Fizz Dog and Beamer Boy were definitely missing their daily walks.

My back hadn't been right for years. I had first done it serious damage during a heavy session of vaulting exercises during a promotional PTI course a few years back. I had been 30 at the time but had, for some reason, imagined I was still 20. Filled with gung-ho spirit, I had attempted the dreaded triple cross box vault, a favourite challenge of the PT staff and one that nearly always resulted in a crumpled PTI lying on the far side of the three boxes, face down on the thin green landing mat. Sure enough, that's what had happened to me. I could still remember – and feel – the thud.

But I had always assumed my back pain would never get any worse. I had tried to keep on top of it by maintaining my core strength with exercises and posture training, but it had probably been Afghanistan that had done for it. Running round there for six months with the standard heavy backpack couldn't have helped. The combined weight of the mortar bombs, radio batteries, ammunition and water had probably weighed around 30 kilograms, and that didn't take into account the heavy body armour and combat helmet that were the compulsory fashion accessories for the posting.

The medical board was a real worry. It would involve me going before a board of high-ranking military doctors and surgeons. If they deemed that I was beyond repair, then there would be no sentiment or sympathy shown. I would be packed off with a medical pension that same day. There would be no going back to work, no rehabilitation. I would walk into camp that morning a marine and leave that afternoon a civilian.

'Shiiiit,' was all I could think of to say to the smiling surgeon again.

He told me that sitting at a desk for long periods would aggravate my back, while doing the normal day-to-day hard-man stuff that marines did would definitely make it worse, too. And I knew the military would not want to take responsibility for aggravating the situation now that they had identified it.

The Marines didn't have a lot of other day jobs that I could easily fit into with my seniority and specialised training as a PTI.

I hobbled out into the waiting room where I stood upright against the wall; sitting down in the hard chairs would be a non-starter. Lisa was due to collect me in about 15 minutes. She had used some of her sea leave to run me into the unit sick bay for the test results.

I looked round the sick bay waiting room at the nervously waiting, wide-eyed recruits, the uniforms ill-fitting and baggy over their mostly skinny teenage frames. Most were fresh from their first extremely short military-grade haircuts.

They were all due their confirmation dental and medical checks. Officially, they had been recruits for two days of a potential 22-year career.

I remembered the day it had all started for me, 2nd February 1988. I could still remember knocking out 150 press-ups in my smart shirt and trousers on the train platform that served as the recruit depot of the Marines. I had answered the roll call but forgotten to address the marine greeting us as 'Corporal'. His revenge had been to issue press-ups.

There had then followed 30 weeks of mostly physical hell, but it had been worth it to claim the coveted green beret that was the mark of a Royal Marine Commando. But as I watched the recruits jump up as their names were called by the naval orderly, I knew that my time was at an end. I had a fairly good idea that I was soon going to be plain Mr Farthing again.

I didn't feel upset. I knew it had to end some time. I just hadn't counted on being broken when it happened.

Lisa used another day of her sea leave to drive me to Portsmouth, to the HQ of the medical board. Back in my office, everything I owned was packed up and my desk cleared. I had been in work on and off for the best part of three weeks, getting everything in order and leaving handover notes to whoever would be taking on my job if the medical board said my time was over.

The top of the desk was clear, but the boxes under the table were full of my current 'To do' projects. I couldn't help but snigger as I thought of the short-lived sense of relief that the marine who would next sit behind this desk would feel as he walked into the office for the first time.

Our dog pack was happily sitting in the rear of the van enjoying the drive as we chugged along with the morning traffic on the dual carriageway towards the south coast.

'What the hell am I going to do if they kick me out?' I asked Lisa for the hundredth time as I shifted positions again, the painkillers still not strong enough.

'Well, for a start you can spend time cracking on with all of the charity admin,' Lisa said, as she turned her head to smile quickly in my direction.

'Yeah, but that doesn't pay the bills,' I reminded her.

It was something of which I was all too painfully aware. As trustees of the charity, we could not claim a daily wage for our time and effort: not that we wanted to. But now I didn't have an income as such, it would make things slightly more difficult.

'It'll be okay,' Lisa replied without taking her eyes from the road this time. 'Something'll come up.'

I suppose deep down I shared her optimism. We normally just got on with things and we weren't the types to worry unduly. But as I watched the fields and lanes of Hampshire fly by, it was hard not to be aware of the ever-tightening knot in my stomach.

As I walked down the wide, dark, wood-panelled corridor, the pain in my back was, for a moment at least, forgotten. An officer ushered me into the room where the board sat and I took a deep breath.

'Okay, Farthing, this it,' I said to myself.

As I took a seat, a row of stern faces stared at me from across the long, wooden table, gold-braided uniforms offering the only hint of colour in the otherwise austere room.

Piles of reports and recommendations were stacked high in front of each of the senior officers that made up the committee. They weren't all about me, of course. I was just one of over 30 people attending the board that day. Some of them had sustained injuries in combat, rather than through contact with a filing cabinet, but we would all be treated the same way. The board's job wasn't exactly that glamorous, and their emotionless faces told me that they had seen it all before.

The interview didn't last long, and I assumed they had already made their decision long before I had entered the stale-smelling room.

From what the surgeon had told me, there was no way my back was going to get any better. I knew from long experience of seeing other mates discharged through injuries that the Forces couldn't afford to carry anyone who wasn't 100 per cent up to the job. A physical-training instructor who couldn't bend down to tie his shoelaces let alone manage a sit-up was about as much use as a chocolate teapot, and I had no intention of taking up a welfare post. I wasn't cut out to sit and chat to disgruntled wives over a cup of tea as they moaned about their other half being away on exercise yet again. I knew there was more to it than that, but either way I wasn't cut out for the softly softly approach.

And yet there was still a part of me that was disappointed when they announced their very simple decision. 'Colour Sergeant Farthing, we find that you are unfit for further duty, and rule that you are to be medically discharged from the Royal Marines with immediate effect,' the senior member of the board said, completely unemotionally. 'We would like to thank you for your service to Her Majesty.'

'With immediate effect' meant exactly that. I was to leave immediately. The head of the board explained that I was not to return to work except to hand in my uniform, military ID card and to complete the required paperwork.

That was that. Twenty years of service over in less than ten minutes. I was now a civilian.

I walked along the shingle path through the well-maintained gardens that surrounded the Medical Board building, my best military dress blue uniform seemingly out of place amongst the green shrubs and small trees that lined the carefully crafted borders. My combat uniform would have been more fitting.

Lisa was waiting patiently in the van on the other side of the car park, with the dogs sitting quietly at its open side. She smiled as I approached. I just nodded and smiled back. I didn't need to say anything. My expression would have said it all.

'Let's get one thing straight,' I whispered in her ear as she hugged me. 'Just because I'm now a Mr and you are still serving does not alter the fact that I still hold the senior position in this family.'

Lisa pulled away from me and shut the door of the van. 'Shut up, civvy, and get in the van,' she said chuckling. 'It is time to get you home so you can start making a difference to the world.'

I smiled and did as I was told. I climbed stiffly into the van for the long journey back home, and the start of a very different chapter in my life.

CHAPTER THIRTEEN

Is that a Puppy in your Pocket?

By Christmas of 2008, there was no doubt that the charity had stepped up a gear. In fact it had probably stepped up two gears.

We now had a solid base of steady supporters around the country and we were slowly getting the hang of co-ordinating their fundraising activities, and advising them on whether they needed licences to hold events, insurance and all sorts of other stuff.

And then there was the small matter of the dogs – the reason for the charity's existence. The problem of finding enough time in the day to actually reply to all the queries we were receiving had, if anything, grown bigger. Modern methods of communication are great but now everybody wants instantaneous responses. Some people seemed, at times, to get really annoyed when it took us a while to answer their queries.

Our list of rescue operations was growing daily, and the number of photos of puppies pinned up around our improvised home office was frightening. Of course, in every shot the dogs looked like they didn't have a care in the world, but the photos camouflaged the urgency of their plight.

Thanks to the newspaper and television coverage we were receiving, the charity was becoming quite well known and really, when we thought about it, the charity was probably the only good news story to be coming out of Afghanistan at the moment. As a result, the families of the soldiers who had adopted Afghan dogs during tours of Afghanistan were finding it easier to reach out to us for help, and our list of dogs awaiting rescue was now filled with a string of heartbreaking stories.

First, there was Hannah, who had been discovered by a Royal Marine as the sun rose on a particularly bitter Afghan winter's morning. The marine had been on watch and had, for a split second, noticed a brief movement at the base of the wire fence that was the boundary to the camp. He had soon recognised it for what it was.

The small brown lump of shivering fur huddled against the bare metal fence was a dog. When he had been relieved from duty, the marine had crawled out to the fence and used pliers to cut a hole large enough to drag the tired puppy into the camp. We had successfully spirited Hannah out of Afghanistan, and she was now in quarantine in the UK.

The next case was that of a small greyish-brown pup that had been discovered in much the same circumstances as Fubar, discarded on the side of an Afghan track, alone and starving. In this case, it had been a member of a platoon in the Parachute Regiment's Pathfinders who had spotted it. He had scooped the puppy up and gently stowed it inside the warmth of his combat jacket.

The powers-that-be had been less than accommodating as the patrol returned to base: 'Remove that disease-ridden thing from the camp immediately,' the soldier had been told. But he'd conveniently forgotten to obey the order.

Paras being Paras, the lads hadn't been able to resist naming the pup after a famous Second World War action in which their predecessors had been involved: the battle for the town of Arnhem.

Arnhem had grown from a fragile pup into a strong little dog, mainly because the lads fed him up on mess hall leftovers. He lived in the lads' room where he was hidden from prying eyes under a dirty wash basket in the corner.

I was delighted that this was another dog rescued from the danger of the alleyways, but I couldn't help wondering if life on the streets might have been preferable to living amongst a pile of Paras' dirty shreddies, though.

Around about the same time as we were asked to help get Arnhem to the UK, we had also received an email from a group of Special Forces who had been looking after an adult dog on their base. The dog had become a source of real comfort to them, but the problem was that she had the habit of wandering off the base and fraternising with the local strays.

The lads didn't realise this was happening until the inevitable happened. Their dog got pregnant and the result was six puppies that were already threatening to take over the remote patrol base. It was at that point that they contacted us. I asked them to send us photos of the pups in an attempt to drum up some funds.

Given the pace of operations they were undertaking, email communications with the Special Forces lads was erratic. But, eventually, I had received pictures of six chubby pups – all obviously enjoying the attentions of the mess hall – sleeping peacefully in a tangle of legs and heads together, on the dirt floor of an old building. It had quickly helped us get a rescue operation under way.

We still had the same problems, and organising travel had, if anything, become more difficult. The current security situation in Afghanistan was even more of a mess than usual, so the driver from the Afghan rescue centre in the north was unable to make what could be an extremely life-threatening journey any further south than Kandahar to pick them up.

Yet again we were going to be reliant on the lads finding a willing local to drive the dogs. We left it with them.

The moment the email flashed up I began scrambling for the phone. As I read and reread the details I got more and more panicky.

'This could turn into a right mess,' I said to myself.

It had been a while since we'd heard from the Special

Forces guys with the six pups. We'd assumed that a combination of their fast-paced mission and the general lack of drivers were frustrating them. But now, according to this email, two of the six pups were on the move. Not only that, they were travelling with Arnhem, the Paras' pup. How they had hooked up together was anyone's guess. But they were going to be transported part way by two soldiers who were heading home.

This had the potential to be a lot of trouble. The guys were planning to smuggle the pups on military transport, something that was strictly against the rules. Their plan was that when they left their remote base for Kandahar on the start of their long journey home, they would smuggle the three small-sized pups in their combat jackets on to the back of the Chinook.

If they were discovered not only would they be in a world of trouble: there was no doubt that the pups would all be put down. But like a lot of plans, it was so brazen that it might just work. Hell, it had to work.

'Koshan, it's Pen. How are you, my friend?' I asked as the phone line finally clicked through to Afghanistan.

'Hello Pen, I am good. And you?'

We made small talk and then I got to the point. 'I need you to make sure the driver is outside Kandahar airport tomorrow morning,' I declared, ready to face the fact that it was too short notice. It was a long journey for the driver and I had no idea if he was already committed to something else.

There was a long pause at the other end of the phone before Koshan agreed that it could be possible. We discussed prices and the deal was done.

The lads were flying on the early-morning air lift. If the driver didn't make it or they just missed each other, the lads would have no choice but to ditch the three pups outside the airport.

The piecing shrill of our phone broke the silence. According to the bedside clock, it was one in the morning. I grabbed the receiver. 'Yeah?' I said quickly.

'We're here,' the voice at the other end of the line said. It was one of the soldiers who was on his way home.

Amazingly, they had arrived at the military airbase in Kandahar, having obviously got away with the smuggling part of the operation. I didn't have time to congratulate him, however. This could still go very badly wrong.

'Right, you need to go to the civilian side of the airport,' I explained. 'The driver is there.'

'Where is that?' the worried voice replied from over a thousand miles away.

'Good question,' I said to myself. I had never been to Kandahar airport.

'Wait out – I'll ring you back,' I said, slamming down the phone and immediately dialling the number for Koshan. I knew I should have been prepared for that question. I had just assumed they knew what to look for, which had been a mistake. Never assume.

Thankfully Koshan answered. We went through the ritual greeting before I could ask what the lads needed to know. The explanation I received back from him was long and rambling, and made no sense to me. Suddenly I had a brainwave. I smiled. It was like being on *Challenge Annika*.

Lisa was sitting up in bed waiting for news.

'Lisa, fire up the computer, I need the internet now.'

Lisa launched herself from bed, saluting as she went. I just smiled nicely at her as I asked Koshan to ring the driver and explain the lads were there. It was just going to take a few minutes for them to find him. It wasn't worth us talking to the driver, he didn't speak English and we didn't speak Farsi.

I understood that the lads had to walk through the reception area of the civilian side of Kandahar airport. I clicked on to the internet and Googled the image of Kandahar airport.

With a ping, there it was. Nine tall, faded yellow tunnel-like structures that made up the impressive airport terminal building came into view, like gigantic McDonald's 'golden arches' Ms all linked together. The main entrance to the airport was situated beneath the middle arch, with the military side of the airport spread out in the distance behind.

From anywhere on the airfield the rounded humps of the terminal would be obvious. I hoped.

The phone seemed to take ages to connect. 'Right, can you see nine rounded domes all linked together?' I asked.

'Yes, we can, but that's bloody miles away. I'll ring you back,' the soldier said, ending the call abruptly.

I had no idea of the soldier's name. I think it was Ben but I wasn't sure. We hadn't had time to introduce ourselves.

According to the computer's clock it was now two in the morning. In Afghanistan that meant six-thirty in the morning. We had planned on the fact that the airport would be relatively quiet.

The phone rang again: 'Right, we're there.'

'Bloody hell, that was quick,' I said, thinking they must have sprinted, which I found hard to believe given the merchandise they carried in their jackets.

'We hitched a ride. What now?'

'Find a way into the terminal building and walk out the other side,' I said. I knew it was going to be a lot harder than that. The airport was going to be locked down and have security, no doubt.

'We knew you were going to say that. This driver is definitely there?' he said, the concern in his voice obvious.

'Yes, he's going to be standing, waiting as close as he can get. He's holding a white piece of paper.'

I put the phone down. There was nothing more I could do except ring Koshan and ask him to ring the driver again to make him aware that the lads were trying to get through the terminal and out into the unsecure area of the parking area of the airport.

It was a big risk. But luckily they still had their rifles. And except for the driver, nobody else had been expecting them.

'I'll make some tea,' I said to Lisa. I needed something to do. I couldn't just sit there and wait.

We went back to bed, but the hour that slipped by before the phone rang again seemed like an eternity. A relieved voice crackled down the phone: 'That was a nightmare. You didn't say we actually had to leave the airport car park and walk out on to the street! We were sitting ducks out there.'

'Did you meet the driver?'

Lisa was looking at me. Nervously awaiting the news as I was.

'Yes,' came the simple reply.

'Brilliant!' I shouted back. Relief washed over me. My heart had been beating like a kettle drum.

It turned out that they had had to bribe the Afghan policeman watching the security door of the airport so that he would keep the door open for their return. They must have looked well out of place as they cautiously stepped out into the civilian side of the airport looking for an Afghan standing by a parked car, holding a white piece of paper. Obviously I hadn't known that the closest the driver could get to the airport was over 200 metres away and through two different police checkpoints, where the security guards had been more than a little curious as to why two Brit soldiers were determined to get to the parking area.

I said goodbye, and hung up, knowing it would be hours before the driver delivered the pups safely to the rescue centre. I turned the light out and was asleep within seconds.

This was become exhausting.

CHAPTER FOURTEEN

The Escape Artist

Although to most people I imagined the twice-daily shifts of dog-walking would be a pain, I was in some weird way enjoying it. My back ached like a bugger when Nowzad pulled me one way and Fizz Dog the other: it sort of became like a test every time we went out. Would this be the day that Nowzad and Tali suddenly adapted to life as UK dogs and I could go for a walk without popping a painkiller?

Sadly, even though they had been free from quarantine for nearly 15 months, they still thought every dog we came across on our walk was their lifelong enemy.

But I was learning to cope, having learned a few tricks of my own. As we approached other dogs, I would make sure I was already holding their leads more tightly, and shortening the amount of leash I allowed Nowzad. He would think he was going to lunge but it could never materialise if he was reined in tight to my side. And if Tali persisted in making a noise, then I would just bend down, making sure

I kept my back straight and scoop her up, as for some reason it always curtailed the barking instantly.

As we sailed past the horrified fellow dog owner, I would just smile nicely, all the while clenching Tali tighter under my arm and pulling Nowzad in even closer.

Today though, I was impatient to get back home and more or less dragged Nowzad the last 200 yards to the front door. He had run out of wee long ago, but still insisted on attempting to cock his leg on everything and anything along our road.

As I walked up our front garden path I immediately breathed a sigh of relief. I had set out early to make sure I didn't miss the postman and the delivery I was expecting. My biggest worry was that he, too, would be early and I would arrive back to find one of the dreaded 'We're sorry we missed you' cards on the doormat. Getting to the collection office to retrieve post where we lived was a nightmare.

Fortunately as I hung up the dogs' leads, I could see that nothing had come through the letterbox yet. I made myself a cup of tea and headed upstairs to the computer, leaving the dogs to settle in the living room. They'd had their breakfast and their walk, and they would all be quite happy to chill for a while.

As the computer blinked into life, I saw that I had another email about a litter of puppies that a group of British soldiers had befriended. The details in the previous emails had been very sketchy and we hadn't been given any details of their location. All we knew was that the soldiers wanted to adopt them and bring them back to the UK with them.

As ever, it was frustrating. With some more detail to work on I could have given them more specific advice. I could even have started the ball rolling. However, I was also slightly concerned about the puppies' mother. As was so often the case, she had clearly been shoved to one side as everyone rushed to shower attention on the puppies. What about her? What was going to happen to her once her offspring were spirited away to a new life?

One of the aims of the charity is to improve the lives of all dogs in Afghanistan. If the mother was left to her own devices there was every chance she'd mate and produce another litter of puppies almost immediately. They, too, would be born into a world of poverty, starvation, abuse and war. So it was important that we broke the cycle that dogs like this mum was trapped in. I also wasn't that impressed that just like in the UK at rescue shelters the young dogs or pups were first to be given consideration while the older dogs were ignored and often spent months waiting for a place to call home.

I was in the process of writing an email explaining this when I heard the doorbell ring and the sound of four howling, barking dogs rushing to the front of the house. We definitely didn't need a burglar alarm, I thought, as I trotted downstairs, although at least you could turn one off.

With outstretched arms I tried to shepherd four agitated dogs into the living room. 'Nowzad, back up,' I ordered him as I pushed him into the living room to join Beamer Boy and Fizz Dog. As I did so, Tali shot between my legs and plunged towards the delivery man's silhouette in the frosted glass.

'Tali, get here,' I said, turning to grab her, only to feel Nowzad pushing past my legs to dive at the glass.

'Bloody dogs,' I growled as I yanked Nowzad and Tali back at the same time this time, and crammed them into the living room, slamming the door firmly shut.

As usual, I went out through the back door and walked round the house to greet the driver.

'You don't need a burglar alarm, do you, mate?' he joked as he thrust a clipboard into my hands and asked me to sign the delivery note.

'Funnily enough, that's just what I was thinking,' I said as I checked the eight boxes he had loaded on to his trolley and was wheeling up the path.

I was pretty sure I knew what was in the boxes: 2,000 copies of the charity's first newsletter.

It had taken me long, frustrating hours on the computer to design and type what was our very first official publication. It had looked quite snazzy on the screen but I was dying to see what it looked like printed and laid out properly. It meant a lot, and it was a big moment for the charity. It was as if it made the charity official in my eyes; here for everybody to see, in black and white, was a record of all we had achieved so far. So I was quite excited about the prospect of getting the boxes inside the house and opened. This was why I had my eye off the ball in the minutes that followed.

As the driver disappeared off down the road, I began arranging the boxes in two stacks outside the front door. I couldn't be arsed with the thought of taking them all the way round the house and in through the back door, so I decided to pile them as close to the front door as possible and then go into the house and bring them in from there.

The dogs were still going ballistic. 'Shut up, idiot dogs, it's only me,' I shouted through the front room window. Back inside the house, I let them out of the living room just to shut them up for five minutes. Seeing that I was the only one in the house, they settled down quickly.

Only Tali was still excited. She was darting round the living room looking for any signs of the delivery man long after the rest had collapsed back into their beds. I knew she'd calm herself down eventually, so I decided to shut the room door once more and head for the front door and the boxes.

I opened the front door in preparation to drag the first of the boxes inside. I really couldn't wait to see how my handiwork had turned out.

The front door was only slightly ajar, but before I knew it, a little white lightning bolt of pure energy had shot between my legs, out through the open door and off across the grass of the front garden like a flash, presumably in search of the delivery man.

'Fuuuuccckkkkkk!'

Lisa and I had developed a tried and trusted 'security routine' for the dogs. It had, so far, proved flawless.

The front door of the house was out of bounds. We only used the back door for entering and leaving. This gave us a safety net, so to speak, to make sure the dogs couldn't escape, and we had installed a temporary gate along the side path that led to the front of the house as well as the main gate to our back garden.

House guests were always given a full brief on arrival at the house. In no uncertain terms they were told the rules:

Rule number one: 'If you go upstairs to use the toilet then close the child stair gate behind you.' This was to stop the pack running up and down the stairs, especially Beamer Boy, who these days was getting really stiff in his back legs after a good day's walk. Running up the stairs, as he loved to do, would only make it worse.

Rule number two: 'The front door is to be kept closed at all times.' There was no outside fence surrounding the front garden, so if the dogs shot out that way they were free to bolt wherever they wanted. The world would be their very large oyster.

Rule number three: 'Only leave the house via the back door when the pack has been secured in the living room.' Fizz Dog was quick, Tali even quicker. If you gave either of them the slightest chance, they could squeeze through the gap between you and the door and would be gone.

Rule number four: 'When using the main garden gate, it is to be secured with the latch and cable tie.' The latter we had added so that the gate could be clipped to the main support post as Nowzad had already learnt how to pop the latch.

We knew that there were those who thought we were a little mad in our fanatical approach, but it was the way it had to be. Fizz Dog would want to escape simply because she thought she was going for a van ride. She'd give up and limp back indoors when she discovered that wasn't on. Tali was another matter, however. She had been born a stray, and it was in her blood. No amount of home comforts could deter her from roaming and I was all too aware that anything could happen to her if she got loose.

As mounting panic seeped into my bloodstream, I immediately realised what had happened. I had failed to notice that not all four dogs had been shut in the living room. I had thought that Tali was round the corner in the bed by the television, but she must have been in the kitchen, and took her chance when she saw the open front door.

I threw myself out of the door, slamming it shut behind me as I went. I saw a flash of white going at breakneck speed along the path on the side of the road.

My right leg cleared the pile of newsletters but my left didn't and I stumbled for a few feet – with the precious boxes tumbling to the ground all around me – before I regained my stride.

'TALI!' I shouted, although I knew it was pointless. She wouldn't come back.

A million thoughts were now running through my head. I knew if I didn't get her then she would be gone for good. My heart was already bursting out of my chest and I wasn't up to speed yet. Thank goodness I wasn't wearing my normal around-the-house footwear: a pair of completely ridiculous slippers that I had brought back from a climbing trip in Kyrgyzstan. With open backs and enormous pointy toes, they were a death trap on our stairs let alone chasing a wayward dog. Fortunately, I had on my training shoes.

There was a time when the run I now faced would have been a formality. But that was when I had been a fighting-fit marine; now I was just another civilian with a bad back. I grimaced as I fleetingly thought how the last thing the naval doctor had told me was that my running days were over.

Not today they weren't.

My back was screaming as I cleared the low wall that bordered our property and hit the pavement hard.

'Run, Forrest, run,' shouted a chorus of voices from behind me. I didn't need to look to see who it was. The house opposite was having some work done on their roof. The two or three workmen standing on the scaffolding had a front-row seat to the action.

'Tossers,' I thought to myself as I tore down the street. I couldn't shout back as I didn't have enough breath for that.

Somebody, however, was smiling down on Tali: 50 yards or so ahead of me she suddenly took a right and shot across a thankfully empty road. Without even looking, I followed. I wasn't going to lose her.

I knew where she was going. Our usual daily walk followed this route, before cutting down the narrow footpath that led into the large expanse of dense woods that skirted our estate.

'T...AL...*I*,' I tried to yell. I was flat out now, despite my back screaming with pain. There was no way I was stopping, though. The stupid dog had no chance out here on her own.

The paved footpath only lasted a few dozen strides and soon the first trees of the woods were looming into view. A whip-like branch stung like a bugger as I hit the tightly packed woods. I closed my eyes and launched into the wall of trees. As I opened my eyes again, I saw Tali disappearing behind a towering oak tree.

'Tali, stop!' I called desperately. I pushed on. Although I had tried to keep in shape on a stationary bike at the gym, I hadn't given my heart a workout like this in a long time.

Fortunately, I knew the path like the back of my hand. Once round the oak tree, it was a good straight of about 100 metres, slightly downhill all the way.

'Time to see what the Tali machine has under her hood,' I thought to myself.

I gave it my all; it was now or never. I rounded the moss-covered tree and charged. With fists pumping, I sprinted for all I was worth.

Tali was galloping ahead like a miniature horse, her normally upright tail stretched out behind her, streamlined by the effort of her escape.

But I was closing: 'Ha, going to get you now, Afghan devil dog.'

And then Tali did something I wasn't expecting: she suddenly just stopped and started sniffing at a small shrub. This was great, except there was no chance I could stop like that.

'Oh shhhiiiiiiiittttt!' I yelled as I just cleared the stationary form of Tali taking in the warm summer scents. But I wasn't ready for the landing on the other side and disappeared into a rolling heap before tumbling to a stop in a clump of bushes.

I flipped myself around. I couldn't lose sight of Tali. Luckily, I didn't have to. As if we were back home when I sat on the floor to watch telly, Tali was staring right at me, about to lick my face. I let her as I reached up to quickly grab her collar.

'Nice move, dog,' I said as I took a firm grasp on it. 'You're a nightmare,' was all I could say as I sat upright, relief washing over me.

I took my time standing up. I was still breathing heavily and my back was in bits. I had no dog lead either, and with Tali only standing as high as my calf I didn't fancy trying to bend down to hold on to her collar all the way home. My back was definitely not up for that.

There was nothing else for it. I bent down and scooped up the escape-artist dog. I then threw her over my right shoulder in a fireman's lift, keeping a firm hold of her body with my right hand and her two back legs with my left. She didn't struggle so I figured she was comfortable.

The walk back was painful and slow. And it didn't help

when I received a sarcastic round of applause as I passed the workmen. With a chilled-out Tali riding shotgun on my shoulder, I turned and bowed to my appreciative audience.

When Lisa arrived home some hours later, the boxes of unopened newsletters were still lying haphazardly by the front door where I had knocked into them. I was flat out on my back on the living-room floor, surrounded by bored dogs, the four of them continually nudging each other out of the way to sit as close as they could get to me.

I had to wait for Lisa to finish laughing before I could tell her about my day.

I was only 39 years old, but it was as if the joints of my back had decided to get old all at once.

Throughout my days as a physical-training instructor, I had lived on a diet of hard exercise. I was used to running for miles, every single day. I would do downright stupid things like running up and down the steepest hills I could find – twice. Even out in Afghanistan in the remote fire bases, you would still find marines keeping fit by using a discarded metal bar with bulging sandbags secured to either end with yards of black masking tape.

The girly physiotherapy exercises I had been given to keep my back in check just didn't seem enough. I felt stupid standing in the living room carrying out my lower back thrusts, and I was glad nobody except the dogs saw me. I had even banned Lisa from being around while I went through the routine. She knew the pain I was in. But it didn't stop her from laughing.

She also knew what I should and shouldn't be doing, so she would yell at me when I tried knocking out a few hundred press-ups: 'You know that's going to do you more harm than good!'

She was right, of course, but I couldn't resist. It was just alien not doing any exercise any more.

I had asked the GP for his no-frills opinion: would my back stay as it was or get worse?

He had smiled at me and simply asked: 'Well, are you going to spend the rest of your life taking it easy?'

'No, probably not,' I had smiled back.

'Then, no, you're screwed,' he had replied, straight to the point.

I liked a doctor that didn't beat about the bush.

As long as I did my daily exercises, didn't go running again, stood up every five minutes or so when I was strapped to the desk answering emails, then I would probably get a few more years out of my spine before I had to have an operation to have the lower discs fused. I had heard that was followed by a 12-month lay-off from everything. So that was definitely on my bucket list of things I wasn't rushing to do.

Lisa had already said that she was going on holiday for a year if I went for the op. 'You'll be a bloody nightmare,' she had informed me, and she was right.

I would be extremely bored if I was forced to spend a

whole year doing nothing. But, for now, if I took it easy it was okay. The pain was there but after a while I could ignore it. I intended to stick with the exercises and then, fingers crossed, I would go back to climbing. It was probably a stupid thing to do, but if I couldn't do that then I really would go mad.

Lisa didn't help at times. She found it highly amusing that I had to sit to wee like a girl in the mornings, until my back had woken up.

'Bugger off, honey,' had become my usual morning greeting to her as she fell about laughing as I hobbled into the bathroom.

More seriously, the state of my back had, of course, forced me to take a different approach to walking the dogs. Walking Fizz Dog and Beamer was painful but bearable. But when I walked Nowzad and Tali, I had to make sure that we didn't go anywhere near people or other dogs. Given my physical state, I struggled to contain Nowzad, especially when he became the thrashing nightmare, hell-bent on eating the dog he had just seen. My aim in life at the moment was not to antagonise my lower back, but that was something Nowzad could achieve in mere seconds when his red mist came down.

And as if the dogs and the pain in my back wasn't enough to deal with, my discharge meant that I had to find myself some meaningful paid activity to do.

I had got the ball rolling on setting up a climbing business. I wasn't going to be doing the climbing for the moment, but I had two highly trustworthy and experienced lads who helped me out when asked. I just arranged the clients. It was frustrating relying on others but it worked. I was currently working on some quotes for a Scout pack in Worcester. They were a great bunch and the Scout leader, Neil, was desperate to get some of the younger adult volunteers qualified in outdoor activities. Which suited me fine, as that was my area of expertise.

I was also putting my former man-management skills to good use with a company called i2i Development Solutions. It was run by two ex-Royal Navy officers (although I didn't hold that against them). They liked what I did and I liked how they operated. At least I could try and put some of my hard-gained knowledge to good use.

The best thing – if there was one – about my new civvy status was that I now had extra time to devote to more consistent training of Nowzad and Tali. Just simple things like making sure I carried around the treats in my pocket and spent time on the walk getting Nowzad and Tali to sit and pay attention to me instead of everything else around us. Sometimes it worked, other times it most definitely didn't. Not even the smelliest of garlic baked dog treat could sometimes distract Tali from the bird she had spied miles away.

Now that I was self-employed, I was also able to apply myself to the charity more, and our attempts to make a difference in Afghanistan. Which was just as well, given the crop of rescues that we were in the process of organising.

In the cold of a February morning 2009, Arnhem had arrived safely in quarantine. The two dogs he had been smuggled on to the Chinook with turned out to be Juno, a tan-coloured pup, and his sister, Wylie, who was mainly white but had a light brown patched-cum-stripy head.

Sadly, yet again, the Afghan rescue centre had been blighted by disease and Juno had succumbed to the parvo-virus. From a disease that a few years ago I had never heard of, it was fast becoming my worst nightmare.

Wylie survived the outbreak and flew with Arnhem to the UK and the welcoming arms of the girls at the quarantine we used outside London.

Unfortunately, the news from there hadn't been the best. One of the girls had called to tell us that the vets had needed to run tests on Wylie. Apparently, her front legs were becoming deformed as she grew, and just below her knee joints the bones of her lower legs shot out in ugly lumps that obviously should not have been there. The risk was that as she got older, the bone would not be able to support her weight, and she wouldn't be able to walk.

I went through all the possible scenarios with the quarantine. The worst case was surgery, an expensive business, especially as we had only just finished raising enough dona-tions to support the last rescues and the quarantine that it entailed. Lisa and I had also topped the fund up with our savings: it was, after all, our idea to start the charity in the first place, so I was damn well going to make sure the rescues that we had committed to were financed.

At least Wylie was in the UK. If she had still been in Afghanistan then there would be nothing that could be done for her. We took the professional advice and continued with tests. For now, I had put it to the back of my mind.

Of more immediate concern was Beardog. The big daft idiot had missed the company of Fubar when she had been released from quarantine after the required three months for entry into the Netherlands.

He was a gentle giant of a dog and didn't have a mean streak in him, but we had to find him a home that could handle a horse that thought it was a dog.

One drawback was that we weren't set up to be a re-homing charity, with all the administration that went with it: home checks, background paperwork, visits and the rest. So I was ecstatic when I received a phone call from the Mayhew Animal Home in London saying that they would take Beardog in.

We had never intended to bring dogs back to the UK unless they were going to be re-homed by the soldier that had initiated the rescue. The way we saw it, there were more than enough stray and abandoned dogs in the UK that needed homes. But I was acutely aware that we also could not have just abandoned the daft Beardog to the streets of Afghanistan once he had tasted a brief moment of human kindness. We couldn't do that to him.

It was the Mayhew who had first assisted Lisa in finding out that there was such a thing as the rescue centre we now used in Afghanistan, when we had almost given up hope about getting Nowzad and Tali home, back in early 2007.

Lisa and I were more than relieved, as we had even considered bringing Beardog down to join our pack, which was probably not the best of ideas seeing as how I wasn't firing on all cylinders.

As always there were tears at the quarantine centre as I collected Beardog for the short journey to the Mayhew premises in west London. Before I loaded him in the van, I let him run around for a while. It really was like watching a horse gallop as he bounded off, his huge head lunging forward with every stride.

The girls who had cared for Beardog had come out to wave him off. I was sure I spied tears. 'Rebecca, Vicky! Stop crying, you blouses,' I teased them as we shoehorned Beardog into the back of the van.

I knew the girls treated the dogs well. They became so attached to each dog and knew their personalities better than the owners. After all the love and attention they showered on them, I knew it must be a wrench to see them go.

'Don't worry, it won't be long before you're welcoming the next lot of Nowzad Dogs,' I joked. Except it wasn't really a joke. With the pace of the charity at the moment, I knew it wouldn't be long before Rebecca and Vicky had their next Afghan dog to work their magic on.

Within days of becoming a resident at the Mayhew, Beardog was the star of their re-homing department. I soon found myself playing the role of sidekick to Beardog as film crew after film crew arranged to get the story of the dog with cropped ears, who had been saved from a life of dogfighting.

Beardog was pretty good for an animal actor. He more or less did as he was told, although the foam covering of the sound mike caught his eye a few times.

Beardog quickly got used to being treated like royalty at the Mayhew as they endeavoured to find the right home – one with a large paddock – for him. We knew his stay there wouldn't go on for ever.

Thanks to my lightweight spinal column, I was only allowed to swim for my daily heart thrash. But I hated swimming with a passion. It was just so *dull*.

Denied my usual way of blowing off steam by going for a long chilled run listening to my iPod, on this particular afternoon I opened a beer instead.

'Bit early for beer?' Lisa said as I stomped past her in the kitchen. I stopped and turned to face her.

'Remember how we said that it wasn't a problem that we couldn't get insurance for the dogs whilst they were in quarantine?'

I could tell by the dawning expression of comprehension that was spreading across Lisa's face that she knew what was coming.

'The vet tells me that Wylie has hypertrophic osteopathy,' I continued. 'She needs to go for an operation during quarantine.' I took a calming sip of beer.

I had no idea what it meant. I knew it had something to do with bone growth and was really bad. I didn't need to know more.

Lisa didn't say anything for a second, then: 'Pass me a beer.'

Even when things got bad, I could always rely on Lisa to be on the same wavelength. We had no intention of turning into alcoholics, but it sure beat running up a steep hill.

A month later and I was in a room at the quarantine, crouching next to Wylie. 'You look ridiculous,' I said.

Wylie didn't seem to mind, and I stroked her head gently. Luminous green plaster casts completely entombed her front legs. She wanted to play but she was on a harsher regime of non-exercise than I was. Even little Arnhem had been moved to a quarantine run on his own to prevent the two of them playing together.

Quarantine rules meant they wouldn't be allowed back together when Wylie's casts came off: not unless we wanted to put the two of them back through another six months of hell.

Wylie's enclosed run was festooned with dog toys of all shapes and sizes; she wasn't short of love and attention. The quarantine girls had totally fallen for her, so much so that one of the girls, Vicky, was going to be giving Wylie a home when her quarantine was over. The soldier had seen the bond that Vicky had with Wylie and decided that Wylie would probably receive more love and attention with Vicky rather than as part of his hectic lifestyle.

Wylie had gone through the ordeal of two operations to straighten her badly deformed front legs. Among other things, her deformity had been due to the lack of nourishment she had suffered as a newborn pup. But she was going to be okay, and with another few weeks of resting – as much as you can get a young dog to rest – the plaster casts would come off.

I tried to keep my visits to the quarantine short as I didn't want to become attached to any of the dogs that we brought back. I found it was the best way to do business, and to remain focused was to keep from bonding with them. And besides, I had another four dogs to visit today.

Wylie's brother and three sisters had been left behind when she had been taken along with Juno and Arnhem for their helicopter ride.

But not for long.

Somehow the lads had managed to arrange transport for the remaining four dogs to the rescue centre in the north. It was great news that the dogs were safe but Lisa and I had spent a few sleepless nights worrying about how we were going to drum up the financial support required to fund another four dogs through quarantine.

We hadn't chosen the cheapest of hobbies, that was for sure.

'Remember that when we have to sell the house, it was all your fault,' were often Lisa's final words as we fell asleep at the end of a long day.

CHAPTER FIFTEEN

Off the Leash

'Clear?'

I responded to the sound of Lisa bellowing from a few hundred yards away by scanning the heather and gorse patches of the rolling moorland, checking for any signs of life. I was on the lookout for ramblers and their dogs; sheep; shepherds; Dartmoor ponies; anything. I was also looking for escape routes in case something went wrong. Which it very well might.

Fortunately, it all looked good.

Behind me, the granite outcrop of Bellever Tor rose up into the cloudless, blue afternoon sky. The coast was as clear as the heavens.

'Clear!' I yelled back towards Lisa, who I could just about see along the well-worn gravel Forestry Commission track that led back into the woods on the edge of the remote tourist village of Postbridge.

'Okay, here goes!' Lisa hollered back at me as she unclipped Nowzad's lead from his collar.

For the first time since he'd arrived to live with us, Nowzad was outside and off the lead.

If I had been expecting him to react as if he'd just won the lottery or scored the winning goal in the Cup Final, I would have been sorely disappointed. But I knew Nowzad well enough to know what to expect. True to form, he registered his freedom by scooting off at a fast waddle in my direction.

His laid-back reaction helped ease the mild nerves I felt. And if anything was to go wrong, I was quite confident that I could easily jog alongside him. Nowzad wasn't going to do a Usain Bolt on me, and I knew he would probably only keep going for a hundred yards or so. And what I called jogging would probably have been Nowzad flat-out anyway. He hadn't had the opportunity to sprint for a long time.

'Come on, Nowzad, good lad,' I shouted towards him as he picked up a little head of steam. But just as soon as he had got going, he slowed down again. He ground to a halt and buried his head in a clump of moorland grass, sniffing heavily before cocking his leg.

It might have been Nowzad's first taste of liberty, but it was a different story for Tali. As ever, she was on a lead attached to Lisa's wrist. After the escape acts that she'd performed, there was not a hope in hell that she was ever getting let off in a fenced-off field, let alone in the middle of thousands of acres of open moorland. If Tali had spotted a bird three miles away and 1,000 feet up in the air she would still have been off like a rocket and totally oblivious to everything – roads, cars, people – until she caught it. So for now she had to be content with dancing around Lisa like a bouncing rubber ball, and enjoying the sight of Lisa stomping her feet and dancing around with her.

His mission accomplished, Nowzad glanced back down the track towards me and trundled forwards again once more.

'Keep coming, Nowzad,' I yelled again, assuming that, with his business out of the way, he'd be ready for a long run. No chance.

He'd waddled along for only a few yards before it was all stop again. Another clump of grass had caught his attention. Stop, sniff, cock leg. It was the same procedure.

By the time Nowzad had completed the 100-yard run from where Lisa had let him loose to where I was standing, he had managed to stop ten times. He wasn't actually going any faster than if we were walking with him. In fact, if anything he was slower.

Finally, after what seemed like ages, Nowzad trotted up to me. I held my arms out to make a fuss of him, but the little bugger looked directly at me and then ducked right and carried on past me towards the Tor. I couldn't help laughing.

'Playing that game, are we, Nowzad?'

It was easy to jog alongside his lumbering frame. Fizz Dog was attached to me and was trotting along like a little madam in a dog show. Beamer Boy was running free around us all, just as he always did, splashing in the gooey mud puddles that littered the path. Together all four of us enjoyed the walk and the feeling of peace and solitude.

'Why can't it be like this all the time?' I asked Lisa as we kept pace with Nowzad.

'It could be if we lived in the middle of nowhere and had no friends,' Lisa replied, as Tali continued to dance around next to her.

'True,' I nodded.

It was a lovely fantasy to think that we could let Nowzad off the lead every now and again. But a fantasy it was. I knew it was always going to be a very rare event: a treat reserved for the once-in-a-blue-moon moments when we had the time – and weather – to drive out to remote spots like this.

The slightly sad truth was that there was no hope that we could ever let the nightmare run free anywhere near a populated area. That would just be asking for trouble. It was frustrating, but we would have to live with it. The risks weren't worth taking.

Such negative thoughts were quickly dismissed today, however. This was too special a moment to be spoiled by 'what ifs' and 'if only'. A couple of years ago, an experience like this would almost certainly have been an impossibility for Nowzad. I was pretty sure there hadn't been room in his past life for casual strolls around the countryside, lost afternoons where he was free to go exploring any sights, smells or sounds that he fancied.

I didn't know for sure, of course. I would never solve the

mystery of his early life in Afghanistan, but I was pretty certain that he had spent a large part of his formative years tied up and confined to some kind of grim kennel space. Which would certainly have been his fate once he'd been chosen to become a fighting dog, when he would have spent the time when he wasn't fighting, in all likelihood, tied to a wall with a length of thin wire around his neck, unable to move more than about a metre without risking garrotting himself.

If that was the life Nowzad had led, then this moment, no matter how fleeting, was a precious one. Nowzad might not be able to roam the English countryside every day of the week, but there would be times when that would be possible.

As I put things in their proper context, my introspective mood gave way to a much simpler feeling. All six of us had come a long way in this past year or so. We'd survived a lot, and come through it. We had to enjoy moments like this for what they were.

Life in Civilian Street was okay. It had taken a bit of getting used to. I definitely had no problem with being a house husband while Lisa slaved away at work. But I missed the daily banter that had greeted me every day I had gone into work as a marine. If I didn't have any clients I could go a whole day only ever talking to the dogs – I had to stop myself when I'd realised, for example, that I'd just had a full-on conversation with Nowzad about the MP expenses scandal.

I understood that currently money was tight for most people as the recession hit, spare cash was hard to come by and luxuries like treating yourself to a day with a climbing instructor or taking remedial navigation training on Dartmoor was probably not high up the priority list.

But there was always charity admin that needed completing and so I wasn't yet forced to watch the endless daytime TV. And I could always take the pack out for a walk in two shifts. One pair would get a drive on to the moor and a good walk and the other two would get to go out around the woods near our house. The following day they would swap over.

Life was okay. It could be a lot worse, that was for sure, so I had no intentions of grumbling. I just wished Nowzad could chat back to me sometimes.

'Come on, Nowzad, race you to the top!' I yelled as we got to the foot of the Tor. It was the signal for Fizz Dog to attempt to yank my arm out of its socket as she launched after the sleek form of Beamer Boy.

But the sight of the three of us jogging ahead of him had absolutely no impact on Nowzad. He carried on waddling behind us, sniffing and weeing on anything that took his fancy.

For a moment, I thought to myself, he might have been the happiest dog in the world.

CHAPTER SIXTEEN

Char Badmashis

As I looked at the charity's accounts, for once I was feeling positive about the state of our financial affairs.

There was no doubt in my mind what or, rather, who it was that had been responsible for the healthy balance that would allow us to do all the things we needed to in the coming weeks.

It wasn't me or Lisa: it was the four little pups whose image had been staring out from our website for the past few months; the litter that had been over in Afghanistan, and which the Afghan rescue staff had christened the *Char Badmashis*, or Four Hooligans.

Wylie's siblings were one male and three females. They'd been named Patch, Smudge, Peryn and Bonny and each one was as naughty as the other, if the stories that had come from the rescue centre were to be believed.

Thanks to the generosity of the charity's supporters, money had been flooding in to help relocate them back to the UK. They had arrived at the quarantine centre in two waves, Peryn and Bonny during the March, with Patch and Smudge arriving in the April, and from the first moment they poured into their pen, the reports coming back suggested that they were all living up to their nickname. None of the dogs had beds, for example, as these had ceased to be an option long ago. Anything more luxurious than shredded newspaper was ripped to bits in mere seconds.

The pups had arrived at the quarantine in pretty bad shape. Just like Nowzad and Tali, they had been covered in ticks and all four had needed a good meal.

But Rebecca and the crew were concerned for them as much as we were and after just a few weeks in their care, the *Char Badmashis* had grown a lot.

The Four Hooligans had become such a hit with our supporters that I had begun doing some research into the distinctive-looking dogs. I had wanted to dig into the history of dogs and dog breeds in Afghanistan for some time, but just hadn't got round to it. I thought it might tell me more about Nowzad and Tali's backgrounds, too.

The internet, of course, was my starting point. How did people research anything before the invention of the world wide web? I zipped from one site to the next looking for some kind of authority on the subject, and I was also helped by an email I had had from a professor at a university, who had taken an interest in the work of the charity. It was thanks to him that I had come across some material on the 'Dog of the Nomads', or *De Kochyano Spai* in Pashto.

The dogs are associated with the Kuchi nomadic tribes that for centuries inhabited central Asia and, in particular, what is now Afghanistan. The Kuchi practised the early Persian religion of Zoroastrianism, which preceded Islam. The Zoroastrians regarded dogs as an integral part of nomadic culture, guarding and herding the tribes' goats or sheep and even fighting off thieves. As such, the Kuchi dog had an important role to play in tribal life and was revered and treated as a senior member of the community, so much so, in fact, that the dogs were fed before the owner's family sat down to eat.

The Kuchi dog was renowned for its skills as a herding dog and its ability to adapt to the extremes of climate that it would face as its nomadic masters moved from one camp to another. Loyal, fierce, intelligent and extremely tough, these dogs would have been vital to the survival of the tribe.

It was really interesting stuff to read and I found it hard to believe that this was the same Afghanistan that was now associated with such cruelty to animals, especially dogs, even if it had occurred hundreds of years ago.

As I compared the photos I had been sent of Wylie's siblings with some of the images I had found on the internet, I had no doubt that the *Char Badmashis* were Kuchi mountain dogs.

The four playful pups were identical to some of the images I had seen. What was even more exciting, however, were the breed descriptions I had begun reading. These suggested to me that Nowzad and Tali were probably descendants of the ancient Kuchi dogs, too, but that the two of them were probably more desert Kuchi than the larger, mountain variety that the *Char Badmashis* had descended from.

The research was a classic way of getting time-suckered, but the more I found out, the more I wanted to know. Hours would slip by as I hopped round various websites, reading snippets and looking at photographs.

As I did so, I couldn't help thinking about how all this related to Nowzad. Now I could see where he had inherited his ability to survive when we had been back in Afghanistan. Those winter nights had been harsh to say the least, but Nowzad had shivered his way through them long before I had arrived on the scene.

But by far the most interesting thing were the grainy pictures I found on the internet of the Kuchi dogs. They were all strapping, muscular dogs, guarding flocks of skinny goats amidst barren mountain plains.

The thing that really caught my eye, however, was the fact all were missing their ears and tails.

When I had first discovered Nowzad, I had been shocked and appalled at his treatment. I had assumed it was part of some barbaric tradition connected to dogfighting: a way of making dogs less easy to catch hold of during a contest. These images made me rethink this. Now, although I didn't agree with it, I could see why it had been carried out. The nomadic tribes were obviously a practical and tough people:

they had to be. For most of their lives they were on their own as, except for traditional medicine, nobody was there to help if they became ill. And they could not allow their dogs, which were vital to their own survival, to become injured or ill.

Looking at the pictures of the *Char Badmashis*, I could see that all four bundles of fun had over-sized long, floppy ears with long thin wagging tails: ideal for trapping between rocks or ripping on the sharp thorn bushes that covered Afghanistan's mountain hillsides. Just the same as we docked working dogs' tails in the UK, the Kuchi nomads had docked the ears and tails of their dogs as puppies, presumably to stop unwanted injuries in later life.

I supposed they had a point. Anybody who has owned a dog that has torn its ear or tail will know what a bugger it is to stop the bleeding: Beamer Boy was a nightmare for it when he disappeared into the hedgerows surrounding the fields on our daily walks.

Need had driven the Kuchi people, and presumably the more modern Afghans were just following an old tradition. Who was I to argue with another culture, particularly one I barely understood?

Suddenly I found myself completely re-evaluating Nowzad. There was more to his story than I had imagined.

'I would love to know where you came from, Nowzad,' I whispered down to him now. I tried to imagine him as a frail puppy but it was just impossible. To me, Nowzad was and always would be the Nowzad that I had found in the ruined mud-built compound. Frightened but strong-headed at the same time.

Reading about the Kuchi dogs, I also gained an insight into Nowzad's personality, one that I hadn't really thought about before. Just as Fizz Dog's love of squirrel chasing was hardwired into her DNA, so too the personality of the Kuchi dog was pre-programmed within Nowzad. I nodded as I read that the true Kuchi dog was a loyal companion, fierce in defence and almost without comparison in its deep bond with its fellow pack members. So far, so Nowzad.

Tali, too, just like Nowzad, was fiercely loyal, but again, like Nowzad, would always have her hang-ups. Being the right little madam she was, it was always she that decided if Nowzad should play with her. Even though most of the time he enjoyed their sessions of rolling round the living-room floor, he would sometimes be forced to let out an aggressive warning bark when she got too annoying. It always made Tali jump back with lightning speed, the hackles along the back of her neck immediately standing upright. At this, she would launch back at Nowzad with a series of screaming yelps and bared teeth as if to say, 'How dare you scare me like that!'

I could definitely see that Tali had given as good as she got on the streets of Afghanistan. She resembled her name-sake all right: she was a right little fighter.

As I scrolled down the page of yet another site, I got a nasty wake-up call, however. 'Oh shit,' I said to the computer screen as I read out loud: 'The Kuchi is prone to aggression towards most other dogs and other humans who encroach on their territory, which can extend a long way beyond their actual home.'

The site also said that the Kuchi dog was incompatible with the western way of life.

'Now you bloody tell me,' I said in mock disgust to the screen.

CHAPTER SEVENTEEN

Chilling Out

The sunlight streamed through the open kitchen door. Right angles of shadow formed across what I liked to think were spotless work surfaces, looking as if they had arrived only yesterday from the factory. The old marine in me was still standing rounds, awaiting the dreaded inspection from the long-haired Sergeant Major when she arrived home from work.

The cool autumn breeze fanned my face as I sat in the pink canvas chair in the middle of the kitchen, a vantage point from where I could keep watch over the goings-on in the garden.

For the moment everything was quiet.

Nowzad was in his usual place whenever I sat down in the house, curled up and as close to me as he could get, which currently meant half-perched on my feet.

It didn't look that comfortable.

Outside Tali was sprawled out on her favourite bit of concrete further along the garden path.

Every now and then, she would half-sit up as if studying the world around her. If her sensitive ears detected the slightest sound she would spring up, launching into a frenzy of barking.

Tali's pointy ears reminded me of Mr Spock's. I found watching them very soothing. They never stopped moving: they would twitch and flick as if continually monitoring the air around her. They could tell me everything I needed to know about how she was feeling. Just like Nowzad with his stumpy tail. The slightest of sounds could trigger her senses, even an aircraft flying far overhead. She would give it a cautious stare while she worked out if it was something to worry about. A low-flying aircraft would often send her retreating into the safety of the house.

I guessed it was a throwback to Afghanistan and the bombing runs of the fast jets that would have screamed over her as she hid in our desert compound as they homed in on the Taliban gun positions.

The way Tali reacted to sounds summed up the dynamic that now existed in our pack. As Tali let out her first high-pitched bark, Beamer Boy would scream into position to reinforce the early-warning system with his own barking. Nowzad, if he could be bothered, would maybe lift his head and add a few loud, gruff barks for good measure. Fizz Dog wouldn't move from her comfy slot in the bed by the front door which during the day she occupied while Tali sat outside. Fizz Dog was happy to let the advance party deal with intruders. We had always said that Fizz Dog would probably greet a burglar with a lick and cuddle.

When the 'emergency' was over, it would be Tali who led the stand-down. She would just stroll back to her ready position, closely followed by Beamer Boy. As she did so, she would throw me a look as if to say: 'Chill out, Pen, just keeping the riff-raff away.'

But today was different. In fact every day was different now.

Next to Tali, and also sprawled out in the mid-afternoon sun, was a somewhat larger version of her. With almost identical tanned markings showing through their predominantly white coats, the two dogs could have been from the same family.

But I knew they weren't. Tali had been born in Now Zad. The big daft dog next to her had come from deeper in the northern Helmand Mountains, and the proper home of the Kuchi tribes. The fifth member of the household was Patch of the *Char Badmashis*. We had somehow ended up with him. I smiled and shook my head as I tried to remember just how that had happened.

I had got my first sneaking suspicion that there was going to be problem with Patch when the lads who had initially emailed me about the fate of the *Char Badmashis* finally arrived back from their tour of duty in Afghanistan.

Out in Afghanistan, the knowledge that the four pups were safe had been a small but significant source of comfort for them. But as they had arrived home and the real world – families, work commitments and new duties – dragged the soldiers back into the fold, only three of the soldiers involved had been to visit the four young dogs in quarantine.

I was disappointed, to put it mildly. I had taken the lads' word for it that they would all keep their pledge to re-home the dogs. To be let down after we'd gone to the trouble of getting the dogs back to the UK was a kick in the teeth.

It wasn't the first time we'd been let down, far from it. The promises of free website design, leaflets and general administrative help from well-wishers had all sounded great at first. But when I explained the reality of the workload that would be required, offers of support slowly faded. I didn't chase them. I knew they had meant well in the beginning.

We were coping, just, and the charity was still prospering. But by the time we'd reached the final month of the Four Hooligans' quarantine, I knew for sure that Patchdog was going to be homeless. That particular soldier had not been committed enough to give him a home.

We see the role of our charity as one that facilitates and coordinates the rescue that a soldier has already started. It is their action; we just give them a helping hand. It must be that, or we can't help at all.

As a result of Patch's abandonment, I spent a long night on the computer retyping the introductory email that we sent out when a rescue request first arrived in our inbox. I made it crystal clear that when soldiers started this, it was all the way. There was no changing their mind once we got going.

I have no intention of us having to deal with another Patch scenario again: arriving at the end of the *Char Badmashis'* quarantine period had made for a poignant scene as Patch's three sisters had raced excitedly out of the quarantine reception to start their new life with loving families and adoring kids. Patchdog had waited patiently in his confined quarantine run. Nobody had come to collect him. He had stood at the bars of the quarantine run and watched his family go.

It was almost a re-run of the Beardog situation. In his case, our only saving grace had been the selfless effort of the Mayhew Animal Home. If they hadn't have been on hand then we would have been well and truly in the shit.

Beardog had been a big dog and a right handful. Patchdog was younger but even bigger. Coupled with this, the reports we'd received about Patch were hardly a great advert for him. According to the staff at the quarantine he was always hyper, grew bored quickly and destroyed most of the toys and beds he was given within minutes. No one in their right mind was going to take him in a hurry.

We could advertise, of course. But that was going to involve a lot of cost and a lot of work as we would have to go down the route of arranging house checks and vetting, taking up time we just did not have. So, after much soul searching and a few beers, Lisa and I came up with the only semi-practical solution: Patch would come to live with us.

We bargained that he wouldn't add too much to the already lively food bill that the pack landed us with every month.

It wasn't as bad as it sounded. Now that I was a civilian, I mainly worked from home. It was Lisa who packed the seaman's kit bag every day.

And so it was that I had driven up to the quarantine once more and driven back with a new member of the household. So now we were seven.

A psychologist would, I'm sure, have had a field day analysing what was going on. Actually, it wasn't hard to work out. As I sat in the pink sun chair, the autumn afternoon gently dwindling away as I waited for my laptop to warm up, it hit me like a steam train. I studied the scene in front of me.

It was so obvious. Why had I not thought of this before? All five dogs were lying down in my vicinity, each of them on duty, watching, waiting for the unknown threat if and when it ever arrived.

My mind rushed back to our compound in Afghanistan and my dog pack there. I remembered how they, too, had sat round me when I dropped in to see them for the odd few minutes that operations would allow. The dogs would wait, eyeing the scene around them, always with one ear to the wind. Back then it had been Jena, her dirt-splattered tail wagging slowly against the sandbags of the improvised dog mortar shelter we'd built for them. Skinny RPG would be leaning against stumpy little AK, whose big eyes followed my every move until I sat still. Nowzad would then just plonk himself down in the dust next to me. Big Dushka, with his bear-like head and thick-set body, would quietly park himself away from us, but still close enough to be part of the pack.

It was as clear as the light of day. Subconsciously I had been happy that Patch didn't have a home. After failing to ensure that RPG, AK and Dushka had made the safety of the rescue centre, I was trying to make amends. It didn't need a psychologist to explain it. I was slowly re-forming my Now Zad pack.

Introducing Patch to the rest of the gang had been relatively easy.

I had imagined that Nowzad would want to eat him, just as he always did with a strange dog, especially one that arrived unannounced in his back garden. But he had been fine, completely uninterested by the new arrival. Beamer Boy and Fizz Dog had just looked at me in resignation and then happily gone out to sniff the new boy. Surprisingly, it had been Tali who had been the most vocal.

As soon as she had spotted him, she had sprinted up to the confused and trembling newcomer and stood as close as she dared while barking angrily at him. If he had wanted to, Patch could have just opened his bear-sized mouth and gobbled the annoying little madam in one gulp. But he didn't, thankfully.

Things soon settled down. Between us, Lisa and I managed to juggle all five dogs so we could walk together.

I held Patch in my left hand and Fizz Dog and Beamer Boy in my right. Lisa opted for Nowzad straining from her left while Tali sniped at the back of Patch's legs every now and again, from the lead in Lisa's right hand.

During Patch's first-ever walk in Great Britain, he had behaved just like Nowzad and had stopped to sniff every blade of grass on the route. But unlike Nowzad, he didn't want to wee on everything, which was a relief.

We had intended to leave Patch in the outside run until Nowzad adjusted to him, and then maybe let him sleep in the hallway with the rest of the pack. But the pitiful howling that echoed round our estate within minutes of me closing the back door ended that particular idea.

We did feel guilty. After all, it was the first time in his life that he had been left on his own at night. The pictures we had received from Afghanistan had shown a contented litter of cute pups, fast asleep and entwined round each other. That was the world he knew. This was very different.

I looked at Lisa as she made a fuss of him so that he knew he was amongst friends, stroking the big dope's head as he sat on the kitchen floor. Obviously he was relieved that we had allowed him out of the kennel to join us, but he was a big bugger. Even when he was sitting down, his head was level with Lisa's chest.

I owed Lisa a lot. I smiled at her; I didn't think there would have been many women on the planet that could have coped living in my mad little world. Lisa was amazing in her ability of seeming to thrive on the job of keeping me and the dogs in check. She organised her days well in advance, which was always a good thing as normally it meant she could jump in and help me out last minute and, as a bonus, she always volunteered to hold my ropes for me when I wanted to go climbing.

What more could I ask?

Lisa was one in a million. She was my soulmate.

'What are you staring at?' Lisa asked, looking slightly defensive.

'I was just thinking how good you look in a bikini,' I replied cheekily. I wasn't about to tell her the girly thoughts that had just been going through my head.

Lisa just looked at me blankly. I thought I noticed a slight quizzical rise to her eyebrow and I finally got the message.

There wasn't going to be a bikini moment tonight.

'Fine,' I said as I shook my head. 'I'll get my sleeping bag.' It was fair enough. After all, everything had, as always, been my doing.

So Patch spent the first night of his new life curled up in a dog bed next to me, while I took the rock-hard kitchen floor. Nowzad was curled tightly against the other side of the closed kitchen door, snoring loudly. It took an age for me to get to sleep.

I don't know how long I had been out when I heard what I thought was the sound of rain falling. My sleep-confused mind couldn't work it out: I knew I wasn't in my bed and it took a few seconds to remember I was on the floor of the kitchen.

Befuddled, it took me a few moments more to find my bearings as I stumbled to find the light switch. The fluorescent bulb flicked on to reveal a large pool of dog wee slowly radiating outwards from where Patch had just finished squatting.

The bloody dog had only missed my head by three inches. If he had cocked his leg like any other male dog, then I would have needed to go for a shower.

'Shit, that was close, Patch, you nightmare. Come on, outside. It's wee time.' The cool night air revived me somewhat and I told him: 'Better get started on using the outdoor facilities sooner rather than later.'

As Patch ran round the garden in the dead of night, I looked back at the pool of dog wee. I had been lucky. Lisa would never have let me live that one down.

I placed the laptop down and clapped my hands. The golden autumn sun had pretty much gone by now, and the dogs all more or less as one sprang to life, glad to come in out of the gathering shadows. I started on the military drill-like task of getting them fed.

I couldn't help but smile as I watched Nowzad, Tali and Patch play as I filled their bowls on the work top. It was a blur of white and brown as they dived, rolled and sat on each other. It seemed that Nowzad had fully accepted the younger Patch into the pack. Sure, there was still the odd snapping of teeth, but generally they were getting on well.

I laughed at the scene. It had been a long time coming, but for the first time since he'd arrived in England, nearly two years ago, Nowzad was playing with another male dog. I don't know why but he had never interacted with Beamer Boy like that. Both dogs had been happy just to ignore each other. But Nowzad was different with Patch.

Maybe it was the smell? Did Patch just smell Afghan and remind Nowzad of his old playmates? I didn't know. But both I and Lisa were extremely relieved and happy that Nowzad at last seemed to be adjusting and chilling.

He was still a nightmare on walks but I could live with that.

Patch dived off towards the bottom of the garden with Nowzad in hot pursuit. It was rare to see Nowzad engage any other gear except waddle. On arrival at the fence marking the end of the garden, Patch turned incredibly quickly for a dog his size, to face the oncoming bulk of Nowzad. Nowzad was clearly enjoying himself as he turned tail and sprinted off back towards the house, now being chased by Patch. Tali, feeling left out, dived on Nowzad as he sped past her, resulting in all three rolling round on the grass, pulling and mouthing each other in a frenzy of paws and teeth.

But I couldn't hear a single growl. Nowzad was not being aggressive in the slightest.

'I'm coming in, dogs!' I yelled as I dived into the writhing mass.

Fizz Dog and Beamer Boy sat behind us on the concrete path, seemingly happy to watch the idiots play.

If anything summed up how much progress we'd made, this was it. Open-mouthed, Lisa and I had just watched Nowzad stroll up to Cavey and promptly sit down between his legs.

'Unbelievable,' I mouthed to Lisa, who was still too shocked to talk.

The days when Nowzie would automatically snap at Cavey as soon as he arrived in the house had long gone. He would still eyeball him threateningly every now and again, but Cavey was now able to walk close to and even squeeze past Nowzad without any reaction. They seemed to have reached an agreement.

This was something else, however. And even Cavey looked surprised by it.

'What now?' he said after a moment, the shock of seeing Nowzad's substantial frame sitting between his legs making his voice wobble a bit.

'I dunno. What about stroking the top of his head?' I suggested. Nowzad was still fully muzzled so he couldn't do any damage if he didn't take to Cavey's advances.

'All right, here goes,' he said. Tentatively, Cavey ran his hand gently along the top of Nowzad's head.

Six months earlier, Nowzad would have had a fit. But today, ever so slightly, he began to tilt his head back, pushing against the gently stroking hand as it rubbed him.

'Wow, right aftershave this time,' I said, genuinely stunned, while Cavey just sat there with a big grin on his face.

Maybe this was the moment when Nowzad finally settled into his new western lifestyle? I thought.

Yeah, right. It didn't last long.

Five minutes later, as Cavey moved past Nowzad to flick the kettle on for a cup of tea, his supposed mate let out a sharp growl then pounced and snapped at the back of his leg. When Cavey let out a girly shriek, I didn't know whether to laugh at him or be annoyed with Nowzad. I opted for the former.

I felt sure we were heading in the right direction; both dogs had come on in so many ways since the early days. The pack had made unexpected progress in their dinner table manners, too, which I had been happily surprised by. Mealtimes had now become my party trick.

It had taken a lot of time and patience, but even Lisa had been impressed. Using all of my former Commando powers, I could now get all four of our dogs to sit to attention in front of their full dog bowls. Patch was getting there but not quite to the standard of the other four.

It wasn't perfect, of course. Drool would quickly form at the edge of their mouths if I tried to drag it out, with Nowzad always the first to break ranks. But normally they would wait for my bellow of, '*Go on!*' in my finest physical-training-instructor voice.

Almost as impressive, we also now had Tali and Nowzad trained to wee on command. It was still a hellish fight to get them out of the back door and into the garden in the morning, but they would do it now, and the wet patches in the hall were becoming rare. The days when I would have to step gingerly down the stairs first thing in the morning were a thing of the past.

Thinking about it, I suppose *that* one might have been the most welcome change of them all.

CHAPTER EIGHTEEN

A Dog in the House

The armed policeman had just waved a group of well-dressed people through the checkpoint when he turned and saw Nowzad standing three feet away from the muzzle of his submachine gun.

'Er, where's this one off to?' he asked, slightly taken aback.

'We've both been invited to this,' I said, flashing the rather grand-looking invitation I was holding in one hand, while reining in Nowzad with the other.

The policeman glanced at the paper then passed it to his smartly dressed colleague inside the security booth.

She was soon handing him back the paper while smiling down at Nowzad. 'Yup, they're okay,' she said.

'Looks like you'd better come through then,' the policeman replied, seemingly still not quite sure what was going on.

I could understand his confusion. We were passing through what is officially known as Black Rod's Entrance to the Palace of Westminster (but what is more commonly known as the western entrance of the House of Lords). It has seen its fair share of unusual visitors passing through over the centuries, but I'm prepared to bet that this was the first earless, tailless Afghan fighting dog that had passed through its portals as, a couple of months earlier, Nowzad and I had received an invitation to attend the annual International Fund for Animal Welfare's (IFAW) Animal Action Awards, held at Westminster in the October of 2009.

With the publicity that the charity was gaining, I had already been along to the Dogs Trust annual prize-giving ceremony in London, earlier in the year where, to my surprise, I had won the Dog's Best Friend award. I had felt humbled that an organisation as big and influential as the Dogs Trust would recognise my limited efforts with the dogs of Afghanistan.

The evening had been a red-carpet event held in London. It had felt a bit odd to me as, for the first time, now that I was a civilian, I was no longer entitled to wear my best dress uniform. I had reluctantly found myself shopping for a dinner jacket, while Lisa had donned a slinky dress for the occasion.

We had been excited to see the throng of celebrities milling round, although it soon became clear that none of them were interested in the two of us, standing holding pints of beer in the corner whilst everybody else sipped from champagne flutes.

It was fascinating to watch: the horde of reporters and

cameramen from the glossy magazines were not to be ignored as far as we could make out. Although it sounds slightly cynical, we did wonder how many celebs had turned up just to have a photo in the papers with a charity logo behind them.

But the Dogs Trust staff had gone out of their way to make us feel welcome and the evening had been a fantastic experience, especially when I had been called to collect my award from the lovely Jenni Falconer. Sadly, I only managed to have my hand round her waist for a few seconds before I was ushered from the stage.

I had shrugged my shoulders as, on returning to my seat, Lisa had given me the evil eye: 'Not my type, honest, honey,' I had said quickly, sitting down to promptly enjoy an elbow to the ribs.

I had assumed that what we were trying to achieve in Afghanistan was now old news, but I was extremely chuffed, yet again, when we were then approached by the IFAW team for the awards ceremony in the Palace of Westminster.

According to the letter, I had won their 'Pets And People' award and I was going to be presented with it by the Labour peer, Baroness Gale, in a ceremony at the House of Lords.

I had never been inside the Houses of Parliament before. And truth be told, I was quite looking forward to the experience.

The only thing that was playing on my mind, as usual, was Nowzad. How would he behave in the hallowed halls of Parliament? Was he going to attack the Prime Minister or the Chancellor of the Exchequer? (Given the financial mess the country was in, no one would have blamed him, I suppose.)

But, being serious, I was concerned with thinking about what potentially could happen if something went wrong inside the great House.

One problem was Lisa's availability. As ever, bickering between Lisa's different department heads meant that she was struggling to get the required time off to attend the event. Even though it was a great public relations opportunity for the Royal Navy, and she had given her superior officer enough notice, they were still stalling her permission to attend just 24 hours before the big event. Finally, at 21:00 hours the evening before, Lisa was given the go-ahead.

The slight technical problem was that she was now at sea.

With the helicopter transfer to Plymouth harbour not until 6 a.m. of the morning of the presentation, and the actual event starting at lunchtime, she realistically didn't have a snowball's chance in hell of making it. But, determined to give it a go, once off the helo, Lisa caught the next available train to London, still in her work uniform. I wanted her there with me. She deserved recognition every bit as much as I did.

I had set off early in the morning with Nowzad in the van, parking at Woking station where we then caught a train into the centre of London. It had taken me half an hour to walk Nowzad round the cluttered car park until he had no wee left, before we tackled the busy commuter railway station.

Nowzad managed his first train journey fairly well. We hid ourselves by one of the toilets at the end of a carriage, Nowzad tight on the lead attached to my wrist and jammed between the carriage door and my body as the ticket inspector stamped my ticket. I was pulling Nowzad's mouth tight shut with the Halti harness and, with the noise of the train chugging along, the conductor was thankfully unaware of the snarling beast tucked away behind me.

'Nowzad, he was only trying to check my ticket, you nightmare,' I said to him, relieved that the conductor had not tried to make a fuss of the dog.

The cab ride from the station to the House of Lords proved uneventful, the driver making small talk as if taking a no-eared Afghan terror to the House of Lords was an everyday occurrence for him. Nowzad sat happily between my legs, his head stretched up with his chopped ears pulled back tightly as he watched the sights of the capital flicking by.

As we made our way past the security gate I began to realise that even if Lisa did get here within the next 30 minutes, it would still take her a while to get through the array of checks and scanners with which the House of Lords was equipped.

Having got through the first checkpoint, we had to pass through a scanning arch. Again, Nowzad received a couple of funny glances, as if to say, 'What's a scruffy-looking dog like that doing in a posh place like this?'

But the security staff were relaxed and even gave Nowzad his own security pass. Again, I can't imagine that had happened too often in the past.

Once inside the Lords, Nowzad was treated like, well, a peer of the realm. One security guard gave Nowzad a ruffle, then announced: 'I've got a fighting dog at home,' which after a quick investigation revealed that it was a rescued dog from the just as evil fighting rings of the UK.

After walking across a cobbled courtyard, we arrived at the entrance to the building where the awards were to be held, and were led into a reception room. The ornate, panelled room, which had portraits of prominent members of the Lords hanging on the walls, was rapidly filling up with people.

There was a real mixture of people there, from celebrities that I didn't recognise (but then I'm not one to watch much television: having the time in the first place would be good), to politicians, charity workers and other prize winners.

When a uniformed waiter arrived with a tray of freshly poured glasses of wine I accepted one with relief. There have to be some perks to this life. And my glass of wine paled into insignificance compared to the treats that were coming Nowzad's way. As the only animal in a room full of animal lovers and activists attending an awards ceremony dedicated to animals, he was, naturally, the centre of attention. Seemingly everyone who arrived in the reception area wanted to meet him.

Aware that he may not take too kindly to this, I had brought along his pop-up kennel that we had used in the Hilton at Crufts, which was where he was now housed, happily chomping on one of the assortment of chewies the organisers had thoughtfully brought along.

'Would he like one of these?' one of the PR girls had asked me.

'You'll make his day,' I smiled, knowing that such treats rarely came his way back home. We had to watch his weight like hawks because if Nowzad put on too much weight, his body was not up to the long walks needed to lose it all again. He often hobbled or slowed down if we walked him too far these days. Like me, his body was letting him know that he had pushed it hard during his formative years.

Some of the guests arriving for the ceremony were more insistent in meeting Nowzad than others, so occasionally I would unzip the top of the kennel and let him stick his head out to meet and greet his adoring public.

Most were sensible enough to approach him with care. Unfortunately, one lady seemed to have checked her common sense in with her coat at the cloakroom, and when she made a sudden move straight for the top of Nowzad's head, his response was as instant as it was predictable. He growled his best devil growl at her.

To be fair, she realised what she had done and pulled back without making a fuss. 'That's fine,' she said, in reply to my apologies. 'I'd be suspicious, too, if I was him.'

As I drained the last of my rather nice glass of red wine, a voice requested that everyone move into the spectacular room overlooking the Thames, where the prize-giving was to take place.

The awards were being distributed to a variety of people, from a guy who had run an animal sanctuary in Essex for 40 years, to a couple who helped care for seals on the north coast of Scotland. The ceremony was conducted by the head of IFAW and the hostess of the reception, Baroness Gale, and the fashion designer Elizabeth Emanuel.

'We're in good company, Nowzie, so you'd better behave,' I whispered to him as I took him out of his kennel and prepared for our big moment.

The announcement of our names was accompanied by the flash of a few cameras and a wave of loud applause. I decided against making a big, long speech. Baroness Gale and Elizabeth Emanuel had done much better than I could have done in telling Nowzad's story and explaining what our charity's aims were. Besides, I didn't want to leave Nowzad standing there like a spare part in front of so many people. I also wanted him out of there as fast and as safely as possible.

With this in mind, I collected the very posh, sculpted-glass award, smiled nicely for the photographer, then slid out of the limelight to await the rest of the presentations.

But that wasn't the last of our official duties during the lunchtime gathering. We were also asked to pose for photographs on the River Terrace with the event's organisers and presenter, the London Eye forming an impressive backdrop behind us.

As we posed under the leaden October sky on the terrace, I was approached by another of the prize winners. As usual, he was more interested in getting to know Nowzad than me and crouched down to say hello.

I tensed the lead once more in anticipation of another growl. But to my surprise, Nowzad seemed to know him. 'I think I remember this fella,' the man said.

For a moment I had no idea what he was talking about. Then he introduced himself. 'Sorry, you probably don't remember me. I'm George. I was a vet at the quarantine when Nowzad arrived from Afghanistan.'

I recognised him – just. He'd been working as a volunteer vet at the quarantine centre, and we had briefly chatted, once.

He was here to pick up an award, too, for winning as Volunteer of the Year for his work for animals at a clinic in one of South Africa's poorest township communities, outside Cape Town. He was now back in the UK working as a small animal vet.

George had changed a lot, but not as much as Nowzad: 'There wasn't much meat on him when I knew him,' George told me. 'And he had ticks in places I didn't even know existed.' He looked down at Nowzad, who was munching away at a new, oversized chewie that one of the public relations women had slipped in front of him. 'He was also a bit of a handful,' he said with a knowing smile.

'Still is,' I smiled back, looking down at Nowzad.

The only blight on the day was Lisa's absence. She had just texted me to say that she had only just arrived in London; to cap it all, her train had been delayed. All she could do now was to rendezvous with the two of us for the long journey back home. I was gutted she had not made it to the ceremony, as was Lisa.

But looking on the bright side, it meant that she could drive the van home, so I nodded at a waiter as he strolled past, another tray of brimming wine glasses held high.

'I'll take two, please,' I said, thinking I might as well get my money's worth from the House of Lords' expenses account.

The waiter handed me a welcome glass of red wine and placed the other on the small table beside me with a grin. After he had gone, I raised a quiet toast to the contentedly munching figure on the carpet and, just for a second, savoured the moment.

As I stood there looking out across the Thames, I couldn't help reflecting on the journey the pair of us had been on. The contrast between the world Nowzad inhabited in Helmand and the one he lived in now couldn't have been greater.

And I couldn't help reflecting, too, on the irony of where we were both now standing. It had been in this building, a few dozen yards away in the chamber of the House of Commons, that the decision to invade Afghanistan had been taken in 2001.

The conflict was still being debated on eight years later. With troops still dying on a weekly basis and the Taliban seemingly just as determined, a successful outcome seemed a distant prospect. More to the point, the lack of achievement I had felt when I had been there was being felt on a daily basis by a new generation of military men and women. But there was nothing I could do to influence that any more. My days of fighting were over. Ultimately, at least, I had achieved something for Afghanistan. In the great scheme of things it probably didn't add up to much, but it made me feel like I was making a difference and that was enough for me.

I turned away from the scene of a contented, complacent London, my head suddenly filled with a hundred images from Now Zad, Helmand and all the other corners of Afghanistan. I saw the people and the poverty, and I saw the dogs. In particular, I saw Nowzad, Tali and the rest of the motley crew I had gathered in my makeshift sanctuary. It seemed like a lifetime ago. In fact it seemed like another life altogether.

I was snapped out of my thoughts by the sound of Big Ben ringing out a few hundred feet above me. I noticed one or two of the politicians draining their drinks and heading off, presumably to take part in a debate in one of the Houses. One of them knelt down to say cheerio to Nowzad inside his pop-up kennel. It was strange to think that if it hadn't been for the decisions taken in these corridors of power, Nowzad and I would never have met.

But even with all that had happened over the last three years, there had never been a moment that I had wished I had not started it all. Admittedly, when I was straining to hold Nowzad back from roaring after another dog on the beach or when I got up from my bed in the morning to discover he'd chewed the television remote, I would curse him from here to Lashkar Gah. But those moments had only lasted a split second.

We'd come a long way together, a very long way indeed, in every sense.

CHAPTER NINETEEN

Life in a Blue Suit

Watching the three Afghan refugees playing like crazy in the afternoon sunshine was a much-needed respite from the task that had been driving me to distraction for the past two hours. With Lisa off sailing merrily round the south coast of Britain, I had been meticulous in my planning of all the tasks I had to achieve while she was away.

First, there were two dogs, Oreo and Brownie, named after what I assumed were the American soldiers' favourite snacks. They needed flights to the US as they had now been in the rescue centre for a few weeks.

Then there was an energetic tan-coloured pup called Ryder, who was already residing in UK quarantine. We had yet to pay his final bill and one of our many tasks was trying to raise the required funds.

At the same time, back in Afghanistan, we were still trying to sort out the funding for three dogs that a female American soldier had saved from certain starvation. She had named

them Johnny Ramone, Dru and Joey and the three little
terrors had just been safely transported to the Afghan rescue
centre. The emailed photos of the three of them escaping
their makeshift pen by bundling over the top of the improvised fencing had been enough to distract me into immediately
sending out emails asking for much-needed support.

And lastly, we had Kilo, a light-tan-coloured dog with a
black snout arriving into quarantine within days. She had
been kept safe by a female British soldier who had taken a
shine to the young Afghan stray. For once we didn't have to
fret over where the money was coming from, thanks to a
fantastic fund-raising drive by the adopting soldier's mother.
I knew I could relax and not worry about generating the
money to pay any of the associated bills. She had already
covered them and more.

The task I was working on mainly, however, was still
driving me nuts. I knew I would have to get back to it
sooner or later so, once more, I picked up the phone and
hit redial to get the by now familiar response: yet again,
there was no answer. And, yet again, I slammed down the
receiver after what seemed like the hundredth ring.

Two hours of my life had been wasted repeating this
same exercise: I had spent two hours listening to a phone
ringing in the office of the Afghan Consulate in London.

It was never engaged. There was never an answer
machine or a computerised voice offering options from one
to nine. For once that would have been welcome. No, here
the phone just rang and rang. Nobody ever answered it.

Of course, I had had no such problems a couple of years back when I had been in the Marines: we'd not needed visas to fly into Camp Bastion. As a civvy, however, I was required to have a visa to visit Afghanistan, yet how the hell was I meant to get one if nobody would answer my emails or pick up the phone in the bloody embassy office?

The shelter was still providing the vital transit facility we needed to get a small number of adopted dogs out and back to the west. But I wanted to do so much more than that. Deep down, I dreamed of helping hundreds more dogs.

I wanted dogs in Afghanistan to be as well cared for as they are in the UK. Although there is still a stray dog population within the UK – which in this day and age is quite unbelievable for a supposedly developed country – there are innumerable charitable organisations set up to help them, from the RSPCA, Dogs Trust and Blue Cross to the scores of independent smaller charities that exist up and down the country. By contrast, the strays of Afghanistan had nothing, apart from the handful of unpaid volunteers who worked in the sanctuary with Koshan, and Lisa and I working from a spare bedroom around our day jobs.

They deserved much more.

Eventually, I wanted to implement a stray dog neutering programme in Afghanistan. Not only would it prevent huge numbers of dogs being born to endure a brutally short existence, but it would also help the people of Afghanistan deal with another major health problem: rabies.

I knew some people thought I was certifiably insane, hell I probably was, but this had become my passion. I was going to do as much for them as I could. And to be able to do that, I needed answers that I wasn't getting via email.

The idea to return to Afghanistan had been brewing for months. To use a military phrase, the charity needed 'ground truth', the on-the-spot information that other forms of reconnaissance from satellites or photographs can't provide. Someone needed to go in there and have a look at what was happening. The aid worker who had originally started the shelter along with Koshan did her best to keep me informed of how they were faring, but communications were poor, and there were so many un-answered questions I needed answering.

Back in the September I had made the decision to go back out to Afghanistan and visit the rescue centre in person. I had checked with the staff at the centre and chosen a date. I had then looked into the nightmarish travel situation and, miraculously, found a way of getting out there. It involved a couple of flights and travelling via the Middle East, but that was preferable to the other option, which was going in via Pakistan, which was extremely vola-tile at that moment.

Lisa and I had discussed it briefly. She had known better than to try to dissuade me, even when the evening news threw up stories that made my decision to go there look even crazier.

The people at the shelter recommended I stay at a little

guesthouse sometimes used by UN staff and journalists. I was shocked when, one morning close to my departure, I flicked on the news to see that the Taliban had deliberately targeted a guesthouse occupied by UN staff who were overseeing the second round of elections between the incumbent President Karzai and the challenger Abdullah Abdullah. It had been near to the one I was planning on staying in and the Taliban had killed many of its foreign occupants.

'That's not good,' I said as I sat on the sofa, stroking Nowzad's head and watching graphic reports about the stretchers emerging from the buildings.

My – possibly dumb-ass – plan was that I would go in quietly, without anyone knowing I was there. For the purposes of paperwork I would say I was there as an animal welfare 'tourist'.

I reasoned that a dog lover verging on the edge of insanity wouldn't be worth the hassle to any Taliban fighters. Fingers crossed, anyway.

Rather naively, I decided to try ringing the Foreign and Commonwealth Office directly. I was forced to do this, actually, as the Afghan Consulate's link on the FCO's website didn't seem to be working properly.

I had fondly imagined that the FCO would be the one place where I could be guaranteed some common sense. They are, after all, the one-stop shop for all advice when travelling overseas.

I might as well have rung Longleat Safari Park and asked to speak to the monkeys that ambush visitors and hijack the windscreen wipers: 'Hello, I'm trying to find the website to the Afghan embassy in London so I can download the visa application form,' I had said in my politest voice.

'No problem, sir, just use the link on our Afghan page,' replied the young man on the other end of the phone.

'I did, and it doesn't work,' I replied evenly. I had anticipated he would say that.

'I can assure you we keep it up to date, sir,' the young man replied.

'You may well do, but the link just goes to a holding page,' I said, confident in my reply.

'Have you tried the phone number for the embassy?' the FCO man asked.

Like I hadn't thought of that? 'Yes, and nobody is answering,' I replied, still remaining calm.

'They might be busy,' came the helpful reply.

I could feel my composure slowly ebbing from me.

'What, all day today and all day yesterday?' I asked in as measured a tone as I could.

'Oh right, well, how about you pop in then, sir. I can give you the address if you would like?'

I started counting to ten.

'I live in the south west of England: popping into London involves a six-hour drive or the minimum of a three-hour train journey, and that's just one way,' I said, pronouncing each word slowly and carefully. I tried another tack. 'As you are the FCO, how do you get in touch with them?' I asked.

'I assume we use the details on the website,' he had replied.

'But they don't work!' I said, more forcefully this time. 'I need to speak to a representative from the Afghan embassy so I can apply for a visa, so how do I go about that?' My free hand was now clenched tightly in a fist, ready to punch the flickering computer screen in front of me.

'You would need to speak to somebody in the Afghan embassy for that, sir.'

'Arghhhhhh!' I slammed down the phone.

I knew Afghanistan was a country that needed outside help desperately. But to get outside help from other countries, you had to allow people from those countries in. I couldn't believe how difficult it was to even start the journey to it.

By four o'clock in the afternoon I was ready to reach for the fridge. No wonder Afghanistan is in the mess it is, I said to myself: they weren't exactly helping their cause. The beer could wait, though, as I had promised Lisa I would go swimming while she was away – something about her not wanting a podgy former marine when she got home.

As I left the house for the short drive to the swimming pool, I had already accepted that I was going to have to get a train to London and visit the embassy in person.

As dawn broke over Plymouth Sound, the gale-force winds and overcast weather of the past few days had, as promised, finally abated. In fact, the sun slowly rising in the east was so bright I found myself reaching for my sunglasses.

Not a bad day, weather-wise, for November I thought, trying to console myself. But not even the warmth of the sun on my face was going to lift my mood this morning.

I was staring out directly over the bay at the six acres of rock and vegetation known as Drakes Island, which jutted out more or less in the middle of the Sound, marking the gateway to one of Britain's largest military ports. In the past, the island had been home to a chapel and a jail before being turned into a fort during the two World Wars. Today, however, it was deserted and empty.

The real object of my attention this morning was visible just the other side of the island: the dark silhouette of the Royal Marine landing craft that was chugging purposefully through the slight swell as it headed towards Millbay Docks.

Behind it, a mile out to sea, I recognised the distinct outline of the mighty HMS *Albion*, framed against the backdrop of the stone breakwater that guarded the mouth of the Sound. I knew that Lisa had left there ten minutes ago, and was now on the landing craft, heading towards the spot where I now stood.

We were meant to be having a whole weekend together. But the weather had conspired to reduce that time dramatically as, for over 24 hours, the sea had been too rough to launch the landing craft.

We were, of course, used to it. 'Life in a blue suit' was

the normal response Lisa heard from unsympathetic fellow sailors.

During the last two months, we had only seen each other for the odd day or weekend while the *Albion* underwent sea trials for its return to sea after a major refit programme. The last time I had seen Lisa was the previous weekend, when the *Albion* had been alongside in Plymouth. She'd hoped to come home, at least for a night, but she'd been pinged for duty. My only consolation was that with my family pass, I had been allowed onboard. So we'd managed to squeeze in a cup of tea in the Petty Officers' Mess during a break. Not ideal, but it had been better than nothing.

This weekend, however, we had had big plans. HMS *Albion* had been due to anchor at the breakwater on the Thursday night and then sail into the main harbour when her sister ship, HMS *Bulwark*, sailed out on the Friday high tide.

But the first severe storm of the winter had put paid to that, keeping *Bulwark* anchored and *Albion* offshore. The storm's accompanying 70-mile-per-hour winds had also meant that *Albion* couldn't get off-duty personnel ashore.

My thoughts were interrupted by the arrival of the landing craft. Lisa also greeted me with the news that we had to be back at the docks within four hours, at 1 p.m., for some reason, so my plans for a special weekend together went up in flames entirely.

The romantic meal that I had arranged for the Saturday night was now replaced by breakfast, courtesy of a

McDonald's drive-through. We just smiled at each other and tucked into our hash browns.

I still didn't know exactly how Lisa felt about me going back to Afghanistan as we had continued, by unspoken assent, to elect not to really talk about it. We knew what each other was thinking, though, so we didn't need to openly discuss it. And, perhaps fortunately, there wasn't much opportunity to talk when we arrived home, even if we'd wanted to. The dogs went berserk as normal, greeting us by jumping and dancing around as Lisa came in through the back door.

The call to collect Lisa had come through at the crack of dawn that morning, and I hadn't had time to feed them properly. So while Lisa changed out of her uniform into dog-walking gear, I piled up the dog bowls.

We had to waste precious time that day going through the charity's database. I hadn't mastered it at all so Lisa had to show me how to input the latest donations and pay some of the charity's bills that had arrived during her latest stint at sea. Added to this, most of the letters we'd received from well-wishers would need a response before I left home later in the week; in the 1980s, the European Union had had their butter mountain, but we would have an admin mountain in the middle of our living room if I didn't get stuck into it.

Herding the dogs together, we took them on a brisk walk out into the woods before all too soon turning round to start back home.

Before we knew it, I was driving Lisa back to the docks,

a hastily made half-eaten cheese sandwich lying on the seat between us as we drove in silence.

'I'll try and email you,' I said in the most reassuring voice I could muster.

'Okay,' was all Lisa had to say as she stared out of the windscreen.

All too quickly, we pulled on to the hard standing area of the dock and were looking out across the Sound once more. Lisa was going to be at sea during most of my time in Afghanistan. The dogs would be staying in kennels, run by Morag who we had met at the Just Dog training classes. Lisa would arrive home and collect them just two days before I got back.

'Say hello to Koshan for me,' Lisa said quietly, as if we needed to make conversation.

There was already a queue along the jetty of blue-uniform-clad sailors waiting to rejoin their ship.

'I love you lots, honey,' I said, as we hugged for the last time for a while.

'Go carefully, and don't do anything stupid,' Lisa said. I thought I saw the start of tears in her eyes.

'As if I would,' I said smiling, as she picked up her kitbag and headed off to join her fellow seamen.

Lisa turned suddenly, staring at me as a cheeky grin spread across her face. 'And no more bloody stray dogs.'

As I watched her walk along the edge of the dock I couldn't help but think that maybe I was just a tad on the crazy side.

Why on earth was I doing this? Did I *really* need to go back to Afghanistan? Why the hell did I want to risk the great life Lisa and I had together for a bunch of mangy stray dogs in a country that most people couldn't find on a map, much less gave a damn about?

The answer to that, of course, was simple. It was the same answer that I was sure drove countless animal welfare and charity volunteers the world over: we all wanted to make a difference.

I had also joined the Marines to make a difference, although then it had been by fighting bad guys. Now it was by attempting to educate them. Who'd have thought it?

Walking away from the charity now, knowing that I had given Nowzad and Tali a decent life and leaving it at that, would have been easy. But as Lisa and most of the people who know me realised, I rarely take the easy option.

'Time to put my game head on then,' I said to nobody in particular as I put the van into reverse, while Lisa disappeared down into the hold of the landing craft that would soon be taking her back out to sea.

CHAPTER TWENTY

Ground Truth

'Crap, I had forgotten how cold it gets,' I thought, the bitter wind biting into my bare hands as I stood on the cracked concrete roof of the guesthouse, looking out over the mismatched, ramshackle collection of buildings. They looked as if they had seen better times, which, of course, they had.

This view of the snow-capped Hindu Kush mountains looked just as beautiful as they had when I had stood in Helmand Province looking at them from the south and imagining an Afghanistan free of war: a country where I could operate a mountain-climbing business utilising the skills of the local Afghans. I had spent many a lost hour fantasising about how western tourists would flock to climb in this beautiful region, staying in traditional dwellings, gathering at night round wood fires while bubbling pots of goat or sheep stew simmered away, not a laptop or mobile phone in sight.

'Except that isn't going to happen for a long time,' I sighed, as I turned away and carefully negotiated the unfinished flight of concrete steps down to meet my Afghan driver, for what was almost certainly going to be a short but eventful drive.

Finally, after nearly three years of a relationship based on trust and gratitude, I was going to visit the only companion animal shelter in Afghanistan and get answers and ideas on how to move our Afghan charity forward.

I left England as the windswept November nights were arriving early each day, the long flight to Afghanistan definitely an eye opener to say the least.

The fact that my plane belonged to a company that was on the list of airlines that were not allowed to operate within the European Union due to safety fears hadn't left me brimming with confidence that I would actually make it in one piece. And my confidence had hardly been bolstered as I had boarded the ageing aircraft on the runway at the Middle-Eastern airport where I had flown in from London earlier that day. Being the only westerner aboard, I had stood out like a sore thumb.

Save for the two air stewardesses, we were definitely lacking in female passengers. I could only see one, and she was dressed from head to toe in a black burka, only her eyes visible through a narrow, rectangular slit in the material covering her face. I had noticed her at passport control at our stopover in Dubai, where the check-in procedure she'd had to go through had certainly raised my eyebrows. The immigration officer vetted her passport photo but at no time actually asked her to lift her veil. It could have been anyone under there: Osama Bin Laden, Lady Ga Ga, anyone. If it wasn't so serious I would have laughed.

The moment we began our descent into Afghanistan, almost all the passengers burst out of their seats, ready to retrieve their belongings before we came in to land. Again I had to laugh to myself as I watched the two smartly dressed female attendants failing miserably to order the passengers back into their seats. As a knowing grin spread across my face, the nearest air stewardess had turned to look at me, seen that my seat belt was fastened securely over my lap, shaken her head and given me the typical 'Why do we bother?' shrug.

I guessed this wasn't her first Afghan flight.

As I had been reminded of immediately by this flight, Afghanistan remains a male-dominated society, and the Afghani passengers onboard the flight had no intention of listening to a woman telling them to return to their seats. My smile turned to chuckles – along with the stewardess's – as most of the standing passengers in the aisles were thrown around as the plane's wheels thudded on to the tarmac of the runway with a bounce or two.

I had arranged to meet my driver on the other side of Customs and had reconfirmed our meeting by sending him a prearranged coded message. But the chaos and complete disorganisation of the customs hall was such that it took me an age to get through. By the time I emerged into the main airport building, there was no sign of my driver at the prearranged pick-up point – the entrance to the airport parking.

Not the best of starts, I said to myself.

I used my phone to text my driver, asking him where he was. Fifteen anxious minutes followed while I stood amongst the crowd of Afghan men dressed in their traditional grey or white dishdasha robes as we all waited for our respective pick-ups. I noticed that most of my bearded fellow travellers were either openly staring at me or definitely talking about me. My senses were on full alert.

'*Shit*,' I thought, more than once. Here I was in Afghanistan, completely on my own, with no weapon and zero idea of who was actually collecting me. One word sprang to mind: idiot.

Finally, my phone bleeped to alert me that the driver had replied. He, too, was in the car park but on the opposite side. He texted that he'd come and find me.

As I stood there in the crowd, a 20-something Afghan dressed in a smart, western-style suit approached me, smiling: 'You all right, mate?' he said in a deep Brummie accent that totally threw me.

For a second I was speechless. 'Yeah, fine, thanks,' I eventually stammered as I stared at him.

'You know where you're going, right?' he asked.

I hoped it was a question and not a statement of fact.

'Yeah, of course,' I said, without giving too much away. 'I have a driver picking me up, thanks.'

'That's good: you don't want to be taking lifts from just anyone out here, mate,' he said, still smiling.

'Don't worry,' I replied, still a little surprised. 'My mum told me not to get lifts with strangers.'

The guy laughed. 'I'm here on holiday seeing relatives, in case you were wondering,' he said.

I nodded and we both smiled and shook hands.

'Stay safe.'

'You too,' I said as he turned and blended back into the hum of the chatting and laughing Afghans.

My driver arrived ten minutes later and introduced himself as Mohammad. Tall and well dressed, I guessed he was in his mid-thirties, his hair jet black. And he was clean-shaven. I smiled to myself. I had spent the last two weeks trying to grow a pathetic excuse for a beard so I would blend in and not be too out of place as an obvious westerner wandering around Afghanistan.

'Hoofing,' I muttered under my breath.

He spoke excellent English, which was just as well as I speak no Farsi whatsoever. We shook hands and exchanged the password that I had sent to his phone earlier. It was my way of knowing he was legit.

I had used some of my old-and-bold former Marine contacts, who were now serving as security guards in Afghanistan, to secure the services of a trusted local. I had wanted somebody who knew the area I wanted to go to and who would also be fully aware of the need for security: in particular, mine. I had been assured that Mohammad was that man.

I jumped into the passenger seat of his battered black

estate car but I didn't bother with the seat belt, just in case I needed to make a hasty exit from the car.

As we left the car park we drove past a Soviet fighter jet that had been mounted in a take-off position to mark the entrance to the airport. A small sandbagged sentry position had been built underneath it. My driver gleefully informed me it was a captured trophy of the Mujahideen. It looked pretty impressive but I was more interested in the scenery of today's Afghanistan.

It was more or less as I had left it two and a half years before. Rubbish was still piled randomly along the side of the roads as we drove along, dodging pot holes, people, wandering goats and other cars.

There was clearly no need for driving lessons, let alone the passing of any form of compulsory test before you got behind the wheel of an Afghan car. More than once I braced myself against the dashboard in anticipation of the head-on collision that seemed certain to happen any moment. Each time, at the last moment, either my driver or the oncoming car would serve suddenly to avoid each other. Every now and again we would skim an Afghan riding a battered push-bike through the throng of vehicles that were driving in all directions. Rather them than me, I thought.

Then 'Cow!' I blurted out as we narrowly avoided an elderly Afghan gent casually leading his black-and-white cow by the side of the busy road we were travelling along.

'It's okay,' Mohammad laughed as we passed within a whisker of the slow-moving animal.

'Sorry,' I said with just a hint of embarrassment. 'We don't often see cows walking down a road in England.'

To distract myself, I looked at the row upon row of garages built with desert mud that lined the sides of the road. Their wide metal shutters were pulled up, allowing the vendor to display all manner of goods, which were spilling out on to the rubbish-strewn ground. The displays of colourful fresh fruits and bright cloths offered a complete contrast to the bland yellowish desert colour of everything else.

As we drove, I gradually began to forget my concerns about being unarmed and alone in a war zone, as a growing feeling of complete helplessness overwhelmed me.

On the edge of the road as we drove through the populated areas, I could see lines of Afghan men standing, practically in line to be run over, all blatantly waving the bare stump of an amputated arm or sitting in a heap on the damp ground displaying the trouser leg that would have covered a leg or foot had it still been there. As other Afghans walked by, the amputees would hold out a hand in the universal begging gesture. I saw no response. At one point I counted ten old Afghanis gesturing for food.

Along with the blight of the millions of unrecovered land mines, begging was another legacy of the failed Soviet invasion of 1979.

Everywhere we looked, it seemed, there were images of squalor and helplessness. I winced as we swerved round a woman standing in the middle of the road. She was covered from head to toe in the traditional faded blue burka. In one arm she held a bundle of cloth that I knew contained a small child. Her free hand was held out towards the cars as they drove by.

In rural Afghanistan, the husband is the breadwinner and the women don't work. In fact, there aren't many jobs for women even if one wanted to work. This means that if her husband dies then the mourning wife has no choice but to beg to survive, if there is no extended family to turn to.

I wanted Mohammad to stop so that I could give the woman something. But I immediately suppressed the thought. I knew we would be swamped by begging Afghanis and whoever else happened to notice a westerner alone in this part of town. How could I give her something and not do the same for everyone else I'd seen? As a gesture it was probably extremely dangerous, and it wouldn't solve the problem: not for more than a day or so, at least. I felt over-whelmingly useless.

I thought of all my possessions and things that I treasured back home: a favourite CD, my best climbing jacket. I knew that it was all pretty irrelevant in the grand scheme of things.

I was suddenly reminded of what Harry my Afghani 'terp', or interpreter, back in Helmand Province, had said to me on the outskirts of the barren village of Barackzai when I was out there on my last active duty posting with the Marines.

Between us, we had failed to convince the local school teacher to take the school supplies that we had gone out of our way to deliver. The teacher believed that once we returned to our patrol base he would not be protected from the Taliban, who would resent our attempts to restart the school.

I had apologised to Harry for the fact that in the three months we had been patrolling and 'controlling' the area, we obviously hadn't produced any tangible results. Harry had brought me up short. He had pointed out that we hadn't been there for only three months, that coalition troops had been in Afghanistan for over three years and still he had not seen any definite benefits for the ordinary people. Deep down, I had known that he was right.

And another three years on, I hated to say it, but still it looked as though this was the case.

My resolve to be involved with Afghanistan instantly became stronger. Maybe I owed it to Harry. He had put his life on the line to help his people. I should do something in return.

We were, by now, well out into the countryside, and the road we were driving along followed parallel to an almost dried-up river that also seemed to be used as the local rubbish dump. In front of us, a stunning yellow building with bright blue archways and roofs suddenly appeared. Either side of the main structure stood two tall minarets, their distinctive onion-shaped tops painted in the same vivid blue as the main building.

In his broken English, Mohammad began pointing at the thousands of grey-blue pigeons that adorned the domed roof of the mosque.

'Special pigeons,' he said as he pointed at the impressive flock.

Intrigued as I was by the sight in front of us, I was more concerned that he kept both hands firmly attached to the steering wheel. I had no desire to end up sitting in the dried-up river bed.

Mohammad was clearly excited about showing me something and, as we drove down the road as it went round the corner of the mosque, I saw what it was.

We had arrived in a small open courtyard. Its yellow dusty ground was invisible as the square had a carpet of pecking pigeons. I have no idea how many birds were gathered there, hundreds definitely, maybe thousands. There was clearly some religious significance to them. Around the perimeter of the square, several Afghans were throwing handfuls of broken bread into the scratching mass. There were even three locals with cameras taking photographs.

Animal welfare had never been a high priority in Afghanistan, in fact it had never been a priority at all, but here was a scene that told a slightly different story.

'I'll be buggered,' I said out loud as I took out my own camera and took a snap of the surreal scene.

'The Afghans think the pigeons are special as they sit on the roof of the mosque,' Mohammad explained.

Hadith, the narratives originating from the teachings of the Prophet Mohammad, often described kindness to animals in return for the forgiveness of sins, as well as extending goodwill to all humans regardless of faith. The

Prophet himself had enjoyed animals so much that he had adopted a cat and often gave his teachings with it curled up snugly in his lap. So strong was his belief, I had been surprised to read a *Hadith* that spoke of a prostitute passing a well when she noticed a panting dog that was dying of thirst. With her headscarf tied to her shoe, the prostitute had drawn water for the dog. Despite her life of prostitution and the removal of her headscarf in public – both crimes punishable by flogging or worse, stoning – Allah forgave her because of her act of kindness to the animal.

Where has this traditional practice of kindness to animals gone? Even with my limited understanding of the Koran and its teachings, I still feel shock and sadness that, even today, an uncorrected misinterpretation of the teachings of the Prophet has led to dogs becoming outcasts within some communities of the Muslim world, and it's due to a simple confusion of the meaning of one word: 'keep'.

In the early *Hadith*, the Prophet Mohammad had stated that a person would be punished for 'keeping' a dog. Unfortunately, in those early translations, the words 'to keep' had been used, rather than the words 'to confine' (you can see how the confusion arose when you consider that in the English language a 'keep' is a place of confinement, yet 'to keep' does not involve the concept of confinement or imprisonment). In fact, the Prophet was actually simply stating that it was wrong to confine a dog, which as a social animal, needs the company of others.

Later translations of those *Hadith* use the word 'imprisoned' instead of 'kept' but it would seem the damage has been done.

Unless I am very much mistaken, the Prophet Mohammad would not have been impressed by the general torture and abuse that cats, dogs and birds face on a daily basis in Afghanistan, and even less so by the sport of dogfighting.

If only it could have been that easy to get the locals to like dogs, I mused, as we left the bird feeders to it.

We sped off down the opposite street, on our way to the guesthouse that was going to be my base for the duration of my stay.

As we did so, we only just avoided mowing down an AK 47-wielding policeman who crossed the road in front of us without looking.

The guesthouse was heavily fortified: 15-foot-high concrete slabs were lined upright round the lower outer wall of the compound as protection against rocket or suicide-bomb attack. In addition I counted several uniformed Afghan security guards lining the roadway to the entrance. More were in various tactically positioned sentry posts along the walls and roof. I didn't envy them their job.

With AK 47 assault rifles slung across their chests, webbing pouches containing spare magazines wrapped round their waists, they were stamping their combat-booted feet on the ground trying to keep out the bitter, creeping cold.

After being body searched, I was allowed through the

double doors to the guesthouse reception proper. Having made my way up to my room on the second floor, I unlocked the door and was immediately hit by the welcome warmth from two fiercely glowing bars of the electric fire.

Within seconds, I had worked out alternative exits and routes if the unthinkable happened and the guesthouse did indeed become a target for the insurgents. My day sack, which was acting as my grab bag, was already packed and would be for the duration of my stay in Afghanistan.

Just as we had always done in my Marine days, the grab bag contained everything I needed for a fast getaway. Nothing I needed was left out unless it was being used: laptop, camera, warm jacket, water, energy bar and phone. A bulletproof vest was propped up next to it. My passport, small denominations of American dollars and the required Afghan Police security papers were in a secure wallet round my waist. Anything else in the room was expendable if it came down to it.

Old habits die hard. I was probably verging on the side of paranoia, but 'It's better to be safe than sorry' is a policy I have followed throughout my life so far, and I didn't see any reason to stop now.

The drive to the animal rescue shelter was just as colourful and sobering as the trip from the airport had been.

The poverty of the country really was overwhelming. High on the mountains overlooking the road stood row after row of terraced mud-built dwellings. It was obvious that there was no electricity supply and, as we passed by two sad-looking mules being ushered on by a young Afghan boy, overloaded with brightly coloured water barrels slung either side of their saddles, I realised that there was also no running water supplying the houses.

Although I had endured hardships serving as a marine over the years, I had always known that it was only temporary. The shining beacon of hope had always been the knowledge that my discomfort would come to an end and I would one day enjoy my home comforts once more. The people here had no such future to look forward to. With the Taliban seemingly going nowhere and the new government shaky in the extreme, the prospects for change didn't seem that hopeful.

We were driving along what had once been a tarmac road but had long since turned to semi-dried mud. As ever, rubbish seemed to blanket everything. Discarded plastic bottles, cardboard, rusting car parts and who knows what else lay abandoned either side of the road as we drove further into the rough countryside.

I also winced repeatedly as I spotted countless stationary forms lying discarded amongst the rubbish: straggly, long-haired dogs that had obviously been hit by a passing car before managing to crawl off painfully to die, alone on the side of the road. Again I felt useless. I wanted to make a difference immediately.

The endless rows of single-storey dwellings and compounds continued unabated as my driver pointed out the various tribal districts that we were passing through. I hazarded a guess that I would be in big trouble should the car decide to break down, and secretly patted the dash-board and whispered nice things to the car, just to be on the safe side. I had also pressed down the internal door lock button with my elbow soon after we'd set off. More than once as we pulled across particularly busy intersections and the car slowed to a snail's pace, I found myself double-checking the door lock. Just to be on the safe side.

'Relax, Farthing,' I thought to myself. 'Not everyone is a secret Taliban spy.' In fact, no one seemed remotely inter-ested in me. Nobody yelled and pointed at the wide-eyed westerner driving past them in the passenger seat of a battered estate car. Thankfully I was just another faceless commuter trying to get around in the world.

After a while, I had the uneasy realisation that I didn't have a clue where we were any more. Getting hold of a street map was a non-starter as they were still the preserve of the mili-tary. But Mohammad didn't seem overly concerned about anything, and as he would have been in as much trouble as I would be if found helping me, I decided to take my cue from him. I settled back and enjoyed the scenery; after all, it wasn't every day you got to drive round Afghanistan as a tourist.

After what seemed like an age, we finally turned into an unkempt, high-walled alleyway, narrowly avoiding pedes-trians carrying all sorts of goods and belongings. We came to a stop outside two enormous red painted gates, typical of the entrances to most Afghan compounds.

Mohammad honked the car horn impatiently as I watched an Afghan teenager walking a monster-sized dog down the street towards us. The dark-coated dog had a simple lead attached to a collar round its thick-set neck. I recognised it as an Afghan fighting dog immediately. His ears were closely cropped, just as Nowzad's were.

The dog was a beast, at least twice Nowzad's size. Its neck bulged out round the side of his massive head, its front legs flexed as it pulled forward against the restraining lead.

'Bloody hell,' I thought. Judging by the size of this dog, Nowzad wouldn't have stood a chance in a fight.

I had read online that the ancient Afghan tradition of dogfighting was sadly becoming even more popular; I had even read that they were now holding camel fights in the northern provinces as well. I looked away. There was nothing I could do. Our charity was not going to try and interfere by telling the Afghans not to fight dogs – not for now anyway – as that would be the surest way to stop generating support amongst the locals. It would be wasted time and effort arguing against what had been regarded as a traditional part of Afghan life for hundreds of years.

Instead, I turned my attention towards the compound doors as they opened briskly inwards, and the car slowly rolled inside.

As quickly as they had opened the doors were closed. A tall Afghani man with a square-cut beard wearing blue robes and a dark brown waistcoat finished closing the doors and stood back to observe me as I climbed out of the car. Mohammad introduced him as Hussein, and he and I shook hands. He spoke little English but we nodded and smiled at each other, Mohammad explaining that Hussein was the day-to-day carer of the animals in the rescue shelter.

It was only then that I realised that Koshan was not directly involved in caring for the animals. Mohammad translated for me as Hussein explained that Koshan was just like me: he worked from a desk in his house.

I couldn't help but smile. For nearly three years I had been communicating with Koshan via email, along with sending the odd text and exchanging a couple of brief phone calls. I actually had no idea what Koshan looked like. But I also learnt that I was not going to meet him now, either. With the up-and-coming religious holiday of Eid approaching, he had left for the long journey to his traditional family home.

He had confused the dates of my arrival.

It was a blow as I had really wanted to talk to Koshan in detail, but Mohammad informed me that the visiting vet would do his best to explain all that I needed to know. I was gutted but there was nothing I could do.

I set off on a tour of the courtyard, which was divided into two areas by a broken wooden trestle. The barrier was interwoven with the hanging branches of a wilted tree that grew from a circular hole specifically cut for it in the centre of the concrete compound floor. Recently washed towels, that I assumed were used to line the bottom of dog beds, were hung across sections of the wooden frame, vainly tempting the weak winter sun to dry them.

As I began to take in the set-up of the centre, I was suddenly surprised by a tiny brown blob that charged headlong from the open doorway of the house that occupied the rear half of the compound. It ran directly at me.

I dropped down low enough to scoop up the skinny two- or three-month-old pup as it jumped into my outstretched hands.

'Whoa, little one, where are you going in such a hurry?' I asked as I held the cute pup up close to my face.

The pup's belly and lower face were covered in dusty short white hair, but its upper body was a light tan in colour. Its beady black eyes shone brightly with excitement, and it tried desperately to lick my face as I stroked its tiny head.

'It has no name yet,' Mohammad said as I walked past him as he leant against the car. The pup was happy to be carried, its dusty tail wagging excitedly from side to side against my arm.

With the pup cupped in my hands, and its need for a name working away in the back of my mind, I continued my tour of the rescue centre.

At both ends of the high-walled compound were two blue metal fenced dog runs and I immediately recognised them from the pictures of the *Char Badmashis*. In my head I saw an image of the four of them patiently sitting waiting behind the blue upright bars. I hadn't, for one moment, considered, when I had seen that picture, that one of those daft dogs was going to end up in our pack. I smiled and continued to look round the compound.

Both fenced dog runs were slightly bigger than a squash court, and ran the width of the compound. Each housed several small wooden kennels, the four-legged occupants of which had their faces pressed between the bars of their enclosures, closely following my progress as I strolled round with the young pup. In all, I counted nine dogs divided between the two pens.

They were a mixture of scabby strays of all colours and sizes. Somehow each of them had found enough of a place in somebody's heart to end up at the rescue centre, where they were now awaiting the next part of their journey to safety and a loving home, either via us or under the guidance of the shelter's founder.

Dotted round the free area of the compound were two further dog runs that had been built to accommodate the extra dogs that arrived at the shelter. Designed with only one dog in mind, I could actually see a couple of wet noses poking through their escape-proof bars, which wasn't ideal, but the compound hadn't been built with a dog rescue centre in mind. The shelter staff had to make the best of the limited resources that they had.

It took me over an hour to wander round each run saying hello to the various occupants. More than once I found myself being knocked over by overly excited dogs as I knelt down to make a fuss of them. With my trousers quickly covered in the dust from the dirt floor, I soon started to blend into my surroundings. Tails wagged and skinny bodies shook as the dogs in turn clamoured to be stroked or patted.

Just one dog, not too dissimilar from a Labrador, with a black-patched coat, shied away from me when I approached. It was dragging its back left leg, the back half of its body skewed to one side.

Mohammad was still there and had been tracking my progress.

'He was hit by a car,' he called over the fence. 'I found him hurt on the side of the road and brought him here.'

The dog eyed me from behind one of the compact wooden kennels that were placed along one side of the run.

'It's okay, buddy, I'm not going to hurt you,' I said, slowly moving away, keen not to cause the injured dog any further pain as it struggled to avoid me.

'Is he going to be okay?' I asked my driver, walking back towards the gate.

He just shrugged. 'I don't know what the doctor thinks,' he said.

Quietly delighted to have finally seen the centre that had been so important to Nowzad Dogs' operations over the last two and a half years it had been running for, I carefully edged out of the run and firmly closed the latch on the rusting gate as a sea of dog faces stared disappointedly at me.

CHAPTER TWENTY-ONE

Broken Chains

The next morning saw me back at the compound, bright and early.

The smell of cooking rice wafted towards us as Hussein and I entered the hallway of the featureless building that stood in the centre of the compound.

A blackened wood stove was working overtime to warm the open hallway. Hussein carefully lifted the latch on the glass-fronted door and shoved in another log from the neatly stacked pile next to it. With a wry smile, I noticed that sheets of paper with the written instructions for the worming pills that Lisa and I had spent so long simplifying, so that they would be understood by the staff, were were now screwed up next to the wood pile, ready to be used as kindling.

'That will save us some effort next time,' I thought, as I gladly accepted the steaming cup of *chai* that Hussein offered me. The sweet-smelling green tea was a welcome gesture against the cold of an Afghan dawn.

I followed Hussein into what had once been a brightly

coloured kitchen area. Now paint peeled from the walls above two bare cupboards surrounding a sink with a single tap. It was still a functioning kitchen, however, and a large pot of rice was bubbling away, balanced delicately on a stove fuelled by a single canister of gas. Fifteen metal dishes containing rice were laid out on the work surfaces.

Hussein looked at the dishes and made a motion above them with his hands to mimic the steam forming in the cool air of the kitchen.

'Yes, they need to cool,' I replied smiling, understanding him in an instant.

Looking into the pan, I noticed dark pieces of what I assumed were meat as Hussein mixed the still-cooking rice.

'Goat?' I asked before attempting my best goat-like bleat.

Amazingly, it worked and Hussein's eyes lit up as he smiled back at me, nodding enthusiastically.

'Missed my vocation there,' I thought. 'Should have been an animal impressionist …'

As we finished our teas, Hussein led me out of the kitchen and back into the main room that served as the living room.

On a battered wooden door that was currently closed tightly was a hand-written note in English, which I assumed could only have been written by Pam, the American who oversaw the centre. It read: '*Escape artists inside – keep closed at all times.*'

As I motioned towards the door, Hussein again smiled and grabbed the handle. He then ushered me inside quickly, immediately closing the door behind me.

No sooner had I set foot inside than several cats were brushing up against my legs, purring loudly as I bent down to stroke them.

Curled up around the room on various piles of old rugs and clothes were more cats, who chose to watch over the unfolding events from the comfort of their vantage points, seemingly completely uninterested in joining in.

The room was warmed by its own wood stove, which I guessed suited the occupants well. Against one wall was a row of decent-sized wooden cages, the fronts covered with chicken-wire mesh. Little whisker-covered faces peered out at me and I ran my hand along each one so the occupant could lick my finger. There were no fat tabbies here: all looked slim, but healthy.

I stopped at one cage that contained two cats. A black-and-grey striped cat was desperately pushing against the wire seeking my attention. Its fellow occupant, a jet black cat, was curled at the back of the box, happy to eyeball me from a distance.

'I know you two, don't I?' I said. 'You're Henry and Anthony.'

I had been told about these two by email from Sally, a contractor working in northern Afghanistan. She had found the pair when they had just been kittens. They had been starving and cold, huddling for warmth together at the front of the compound in which she was living. Without hesitation, she had scooped them up and nursed them back to health. Since then she had used her hard-earned wages to ensure that Henry and Anthony were going to have a good life with her mum back in the UK.

I had been sworn to secrecy not to let her boyfriend know how much it was costing her to save the two orphaned Afghan cats.

'I'll come and see you when I get back home, okay?' I said to Anthony, the striped one. Henry still wasn't interested in saying hello. If I remembered correctly, he had been slightly injured when Sally had found him so maybe he was still wary of people.

I was humbled to see that Hussein was stroking the cats as they toiled round his sandalled feet. Here was an Afghan who understood that animals should be treated with respect.

'Good to see, Hussein,' I said to him, nodding. If it had been up to the Taliban, he would have been punished, and possibly killed, for showing such kindness to another living creature. I simply cannot understand how a group of people can interpret the Koran so badly and with such devastating consequences to not just cats and dogs, but humans, too.

Thankfully, Hussein had no qualms about the fact I was a westerner and that he could be punished for fraternising with me. He had welcomed me without question and, judging from the way he so carefully prepared the food for the shelter's inhabitants, I knew that he cared for them as much as any supporter from our charity would.

I remembered the photos of Nowzad I had on my mobile

phone and showed Hussein some images of Nowzad playing in our back garden.

'Nowzad,' I said to him and then pointed to myself. 'He is with me now.'

Hussein stared at the screen and then smiled as he made hand signals that I immediately gathered meant a fighting dog.

'Yes, that's Nowzad,' I replied, again pointing to myself.

Hussein nodded and then led me outside. For a moment I wondered what he was up to as he led me to one of the bigger dog runs and then pointed to a spot in the corner. A rusting, broken chain was lying unused on the floor. For a second or so I wasn't sure what he was trying to tell me but then it hit me in a flash. This was where Nowzad had been kept when he'd arrived here from Helmand Province.

Nowzad had spent more than two months here after being safely spirited out of the compound. Hussein and his colleagues had watched over him while we had arranged flights, gathered and arranged the paperwork and raised the required funds. I had been sent photos of him during this period and had been disturbed by the sight of him attached to a chain. At the time I had been upset at the thought of the conditions he'd been kept in, but now I understood: he would have fought the other occupants of the rescue shelter given half a chance.

The Afghan rescue staff simply weren't trained to socialise him, even if they'd had the time, which they hadn't. Keeping him chained had been safer for everybody, Nowzad included. It hadn't been the best solution but the only one available at the time. I just had to be grateful that the centre had taken Nowzad on. The alternatives just did not bear thinking about.

A long way from here, I could imagine Nowzad being made a fuss of in the kennels back home while I was away. I had left him in their capable hands a couple of times now and he fitted in perfectly. The kennel girls always fell for him for some reason; he was a little charmer when he wanted to be. But I doubted he had been given the same fuss and attention when he had been here.

The day seemed to fly by. There was so much to do! As I spent a good half an hour scooping up and then disposing of dog crap from the runs, I was reminded of my time in the Now Zad compound. Back there we had burned the stuff, but Hussein had come up with a more pleasant form of disposal. He buried the crap in a wheelbarrow of dirt before wheeling it out to dump on one of the numerous rubbish tips that sprang up from the side of most roads.

Together we washed and scrubbed out the wooden kennel shelters, which were not the best for keeping clean as germs could easily stick to the wood to be transmitted to the next dog that used it. But they had no choice: these were home-made kennels and getting some decent, proper metal crates into Afghanistan would not have been the easiest of options.

Using sign language, I demonstrated to Hussein how to use the Kong dog toys I had carried over with me. Small, indestructible cones of rubber, they were hollowed out to allow dog food to be stuffed inside. I took some of the boiled rice and spooned it inside, using my finger to pack it in tightly.

A Kong keeps a hyperactive dog occupied for hours as it tries to lick and suck out the food crammed inside, and I hoped they might keep the dogs quiet on the cold winter nights.

As the day lengthened into the afternoon, I finally stopped and knelt down by a fully enclosed dog run attached to the side of the compound.

I hadn't had time to say hello to its occupant on my original whirlwind tour of the centre when I had arrived. As I looked between the wooden bars I could see a shaking, dark-grey-and-white-haired dog staring back at me, his long floppy ears hanging limply by the side of his head.

'Hello, buddy,' I said gently as it shuffled over towards me. It was clearly in distress. Its eyes were gooey and red and there was a green discharge dribbling constantly from its nose. I watched, helpless, as it tried and failed to drink from the water bowl. Try as it might, it could not lick up any water.

'Sorry, buddy, but there's nothing I can do,' I said frustrated. I wasn't a vet and didn't really know the first thing about animal disease. I felt like an amateur.

'Fuck,' I said out loud. I sat outside the run and talked quietly to the dog as it shuffled painfully slowly back into the warmth of the wooden shelter.

It was so frustrating. I desperately wanted to do something for dogs like this. But all I could do was sit and watch.

I stood up and walked over to where the nameless little pup I had carried round that morning was curled against my day sack, which I had left against the wall.

I needed some good vibes and the puppy's excitedly wagging tail was just the ticket.

'No Name' sounds good to me. I picked it up and made a fuss of it as the pup attempted to lick my face clean.

Although it was disappointing that I wouldn't get to spend time with Koshan, there was still a lot that I could achieve whilst I was in Afghanistan. I intended to continue helping out at the rescue, at the same time getting a feel for how it operated under the constraints that stopped it from advertising its presence to many of the local people who lived near it.

It would be good, too, if I could spend some time getting to know Hussein. I had enjoyed the bond that the Marines had formed with the Afghan Police when I had been in Now Zad, and it would be nice to be able, one day, to call Hussein a friend.

Added to this, a few Afghan and other non-government organisations had kindly offered to meet me and offer advice or information about how best to drive forward the Nowzad Dogs charity. Several had been working for years in Afghanistan and the surrounding regions; they would all be helpful in piecing together a picture of the way the country worked or, perhaps more accurately, didn't work.

Spending time in Afghanistan as a civilian rather than a

member of the military had definitely opened my eyes to some of the finer detail of life here. Before, I was rapidly realising, I had been slightly blinkered to the Afghan world around me: I had only seen it through the sights of a gun or as the chosen view of a BBC film crew.

I knew I would have trouble convincing many locals to help me with my plans for controlling the stray dog population, until I had successfully explained how it would benefit the people of Afghanistan. Now I was no longer confined to a compound or wearing a uniform I would be free to interact and talk with the local people, but I could already see how difficult their lives were. The lack of available food or well-paid jobs, coupled with the complete breakdown in security, were all pressures that they had to deal with on a daily basis.

It was also useful to learn about the way the country's ethnic mix worked. Setting up the charity, we had received so many conflicting reports of the cultural differences we would face that I hadn't known who to believe. As one NGO representative explained to me, there isn't just one main controlling political party, although the Pashtuns, thanks to their highly lucrative poppies growing in the lands of the south, and who predominantly make up the current crop of warring Taliban, have probably spent the longest time in power throughout Afghanistan's bloody history.

The alienated Hazara people make up the majority of the opposition, although the Uzbeks, Tajiks, Turkmen and Kyrgyz plus many smaller groups also make up the rich tapestry that is Afghan society. With so many different tribal and cultural groups to govern, it is no wonder the present Afghan government is having difficulty administrating the outer-lying regions.

The internet had become a great resource in my research on Muslim culture and faith. I had spent long hours trying to understand the whole way of life, as I wanted to ensure that the charity wouldn't offend or upset anybody as we tried to make a difference in their world.

Eventually, we hoped to stretch a simple animal welfare programme out across the country, but we would have to be sure to approach every area with a good knowledge of the traditions and beliefs that we would have to respect, but also often overcome.

No amount of research changed my mind about some things, of course. I am not exactly the best person to comment on the religion of Islam. Religion in any guise is not for me; there is simply too much death and destruction in the world to think that there is any great power watching over us. As far as I can see, a lot of good people die for no good reason and rather than waste my time sitting in churches or mosques praying for some greater good to empower me and make the world a better place, I find the time is better spent if I just get off my arse and do something about it.

As I talked to more people, it soon became apparent that the majority of Muslims, just like most other religions in the world, simply want peace and to be able to get on with their lives. It is the fanatical elements of groups like the Taliban that are at the root of the problem. And the main reason for their severely flawed thinking is pretty obvious: education or, rather, the lack of it.

From what I could see, with their own limited real understanding of the Koran, the all-powerful mullahs find it easy to control the subservient masses who know no different. The desperate and needy followers just accept their enforced beliefs as a given. After all, if you have nothing and somebody promises you a better life, what else are you going to do?

The religious schools or madrassas that orphaned young boys are often forced to attend, mainly in the mountainous regions of north-west Pakistan, are run by mullahs whose interpretation of the teachings of the Prophet Mohammad seem to leave a lot to be desired. Generation after generation of impressionable young men are radicalised, taught a narrow, blinkered view of the world according to their teacher's own limited understanding of what they have once been taught. It seems that the blind are leading the blind.

Coupled with this, women are branded an evil temptation, to be avoided at all costs, as they interfere with a young man's service to Allah. Banished from public view under their all-covering burka, social contact with a female comes only in the form of the day-to-day dealing with a female family member, and only if they have any extended family left.

Knowing no different, the young men have accepted this extreme way of living as the way the world should be.

The western world only stood up and took notice of the

extremist views of the Taliban for the first time when Kabul fell after the Soviet withdrawal in 1989. Then, it emerged that women had been banned from leaving the home, even for shopping. Attending school was out of the question. Even music, dancing, almost all forms of the media, were banned and adultery became punishable by public stoning.

To illustrate this, nestled amongst the rocky mountain ridges that overlook Kabul is an Olympic-sized swimming pool complex, built by the Soviets as an icon to their own perceived invincibility. Under Taliban rule it has become notorious as a place of public execution.

The aide to Mullah Omar, the all-powerful leader of the Taliban when they overran Afghanistan during the early nineties, has declared their intent to drag Afghanistan back to the time of the Prophet Mohammad. They want to live life as he had 1,400 years ago.

How was a non-Muslim charity going to change the viewpoint of millions of people? I didn't see how we could do it.

A few days later, I found myself back on the roof of the guesthouse with just a few hours to go before Mohammad took me on the return journey back to the airport and the flight home. Currently, though, we were on a lock-down at the guesthouse for our own safety. A suicide bomber had just detonated his explosives outside one of the fortified embassies not far from where I stood. It was a chilling reminder of the daily realities of the territory I had chosen to operate in.

Where the sun-bleached plastic chair had come from I had no idea, but I sat on it anyway and stared out towards the lonely mountains. I could imagine roaming the inviting ridges and valleys: they were just crying out to be explored. Yet I knew they would remain out of reach for years, if not decades, to come.

My big padded down jacket was firmly zipped up to protect me from the chill that arrived dead on four o'clock every day as the sun began to settle behind the tallest of the peaks. As it did so, my thoughts turned once more to home. I missed Lisa. I missed our pack.

Sitting there staring at the Afghan mountains, I couldn't help but think back to the last time I had sat in their shadows. Back then I had been readying myself to leave Afghanistan at the end of a frustrating six-month tour of duty. I would never in a million years have guessed my life would have changed so much in the three short years that had passed since then.

I had always thought that I would carve out a career in mountaineering when I finally left the Marines: I had seen myself based in a comfortable villa in the mountains of Spain or the Alps. Not for one moment had I contemplated that I would end up devoting every spare minute I had to a charity, and my climbing kit would become just a hobby for those precious minutes of snatched freedom. I would never have foreseen that I would be back here in Afghanistan mulling over how I was going to implement an animal welfare and neutering programme in the middle of a war zone, especially when not many people outside the charity were going to be that bothered by what we wanted to achieve.

'No tea and medals this time,' I said to myself.

It was so different to three years ago. In every way.

And yet coming back to Afghanistan had only reinforced my will. Now, more than ever, I wanted to make a difference. I was prepared to go to any lengths to achieve our aim.

The last conversation I had had with the rescue centre's part-time vet had only served to strengthen my resolve.

I had spoken to him when I had called into the shelter two days before my departure. He had told me that the grey-and-white dog with the long floppy ears was called Panda. The dog had been suffering from distemper, a treatable illness back in the west. But over here it was different. With no medicines with which to treat him there had been no choice.

He had put Panda to sleep that morning.

When I had started the charity, I hadn't even begun to imagine the obstacles that were going to be thrown in our way. But I had found that the more people said I wouldn't be able to achieve something, the more effort I had put into proving them wrong.

I only had to look at Nowzad and Tali to see how far we'd come. Most people thought what we had achieved with them was utterly impossible. They had looked at me as if I was mad when I had said I was going to get a fighting dog transported from one of the most dangerous and hostile areas in the world to safety, let alone all the way back to the UK to live with me. And the same people really hadn't given me much of a chance of settling Nowzad into life in the UK, let alone helping him to become a more or less happily adjusted, domestic dog.

On that one, they were probably right to an extent. Nowzad and Tali are always going to be pains in the arse when we go for a walk. That is just the way it is. I reckon some dogs are set in their ways, just the same as some people are.

Nowzad and Tali don't like strangers. You can't really blame them after all they have been through. But as long as Lisa and I can manage the two lovable nightmares, then what's the problem?

As I sat in the plastic chair on the roof, I couldn't get the thought of them out of my head. I kept picturing the scene that awaited me when I got home.

I knew the dogs would hear me approaching the back door: Tali would be barking, alerting the rest of the pack to the situation, as usual. Beamer Boy would be at her side along, possibly, with Patch. Fizz Dog would be lying in her bed, ignoring the rumpus as ever. And at the rear of the pack would be Nowzad, his stumpy tail wagging like mad as he waited for the rest of his pack to greet me. When all the fuss had died down I knew he would casually stroll over, sniff my legs, and say hello.

I wondered if he would recognise the smell of Afghanistan on my trousers. I wondered whether somewhere, deep down inside him, it might remind him of the life he'd left behind.

When all the dogs had settled down I was going to sit next to my best mate and explain to him what I had seen back in his old stamping ground. I would tell him about his old kennel, and the corner where he had spent his time chained to the wall and I would also tell him about what I intended to do for all his four-legged friends that we had left behind.

Above all, I would tell him that, thanks to him, I knew that it was possible for a small bunch of well-meaning folks to transform the lives of the dogs of Afghanistan and, I hoped, make a difference, at some point in the future, to the lives of the Afghan people.

Against all the odds, in the face of all the doubts, Nowzad and Tali have settled into their new life in what was to them an extremely alien corner of the world. They are now healthier, fitter and, I know, happier dogs. Sure, it's no place like home. But it *is* their home now. They were the first to make the journey, but there is no way they are going to be the last.

Of that I am sure.

Beamer Boy

Patch

Tali

Fizz Dog

Nowzad

Acknowledgements

To have a story that is worthy of being published is a privilege that I will always treasure. But to be asked to write a second book is a dream that this former Royal Marine had never even remotely imagined would be on the cards. I might have put the words on the paper but I would not have had a story to tell without my four-legged buddy Nowzad. He has never asked for anything in return but has always been excited to see me in the morning when I come downstairs and seems to want nothing more than to sit by my side and wait for the moment I yell we are going for a walk.

Without hesitation I would like to thank Mary Pachnos and Fiona MacIntyre for giving me the opportunity, and Charlotte at Ebury for arranging my book into what I hope you found was a thoroughly enjoyable read! Garry owes me a bottle of red but hopefully he is now happy with my inner voice.

A massive thank you to the team at Mayhew International: we could not have achieved what we have so far without them and also for their support with re-homing Beardog. Lyn and the Happy Landings crew have given us fantastic support when we have asked them to assist us with Smudge, Bagzir and Juliet – let's hope the weather is better for your open day this year!

And a big thank you to Morag at Drum Kennels for her patience and understanding in looking after Nowzad and Tali when charity commitments have left us no option. One day we will try and give you a bit more notice – honest!

To all who purchased a copy of *One Dog at a Time* and then contacted us with either offers of help, support or donations – thank you so much. We really would not be achieving so many successes in Afghanistan without you.

To Lisa, well what can I say? Sorry honey. Why would we want any free time to ourselves anyway? Love you always, BBCOMB XXXXXXXXXXXXXXX

Pen F
March 2010

P.S. Sorry Fizz Dog and Beamer Boy – I know I promised no more Afghan strays after Nowzad and Tali but Patchdog is the last … honest.

nowzad d🐾gs

registered charity in the UK (number 1119185)

Every little we do helps, because we are not just walking away –
and we hope you won't too.

If you enjoyed this book, please recommend it to friends, family and other dog lovers. Donations are always very welcome and needed. If you buy goods online please register at www.easyfundraising.org.uk stating Nowzad Dogs as your cause and then click through their website to the retailer you want. The charity can get up to 5 per cent of the sale price of the item you purchase donated direct from the retailer. If you can advertise us on your website or have another idea to raise our profile, please do get in touch.

If you want to read more about the work of the Nowzad Dogs charity in Afghanistan then please visit our website www.nowzaddogs.co.uk or you can write to us at
Nowzad Dogs, PO Box 3495,
Corsham, SN13 7AE, England.

If you would prefer to support a UK-based charity that re-homes unwanted dogs and cats in the UK then we would like to recommend the work of two independent rescues:
The Mayhew Animal Home www.mayhewanimalhome.org and Happy Landings Animal Shelter
www.happy-landings.org.uk

Find out where it all began, in Pen Farthing's
One Dog at a Time

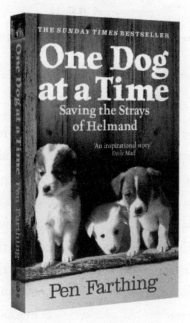

'Highlights how far man's bond with dogs can be tested'
Financial Times

'An emotional rollercoaster that will keep you turning the
pages and reaching for the Kleenex – don't miss it – 10/10'
Your Dog

'The best book to come out of Helmand'
Brigadier Charles Hobson

In all good bookshops in paperback from October 2010

**Exclusive signed early paperback copies available
now from www.nowzaddogs.com**

Nowzad visits the House of Lords

Flying into Afghanistan once more

Afghan strays almost safe

The Kuchi Nomads on the move

Afghan strays scavenging the streets

A suffering Panda